ENGINEERING DRAWING & WORKSHOP CALCULATION AND SCIENCE MCQ

MANOJ DOLE

Digitization is the need of the time. In the future, training in industrial training institutes will need to be conducted using online internet to make training more convenient and easy.
E-books containing a set of MCQ questions will be made available to the trainees as they need to be more accustomed to the multiple choice questions MCQ to prepare for the online
exams taking place in their industrial training institutes.

With all these factors in mind, Mr. Manoj Madhukar Dole Instructor, Industrial Training Institute, Satara, has written books according to the new annual system and NSQF-5 syllabus. And they've created theoretical mobile apps and blogs to make training easier, and made all these educational materials available for download on the world famous websites Google Play Store, Amazon and Apple Book Store.

The books were published by Hon'ble Joint Director Shri Rajendra Ghume Saheb Regional Office of Vocational Education and Training, Pune on 9/1/2019, at this time
Shri Prakash Saigavkar Saheb Principal Government Industrial Training Institute Aundh Pune, Shri Tukaram Misal Saheb Principal Govt. Q. Sanstha Satara, Shri Sachin Dhumal Saheb District Vocational Education and Training Officer Satara, Shri Yatin Pargaonkar Saheb Principal Govt. Q. Sanstha Kolhapur, Shri Vikas Teke Saheb Inspector Vocational Education and Training Regional Office Pune, Palekar Foods Products Pvt. Ltd. Entrepreneurial Chairman of Satara Mr. Nilkanthrao Palekar Saheb, Chairman of Hira Foods Mr. Ibrahim Baba Tamboli Saheb, Mrs. Shalmali Pawar Headmaster Government Technical School Center Satara and other dignitaries were present on the occasion.

Contents

Prologue

Engineering Drawing & Workshop Calculation and Science MCQ is a simple Book for ITI Engineering Drawing & Workshop Calculation and Science Subject, Revised NSQ F Syllabus in 2022, It contains objective questions with underlined & bold correct answers MCQ covering all topics including all about the latest & Important about geometrical figures using drawing instruments, freehand drawing of machine components in correct proportions, procedure to prepare a drawing sheet as per BIS standard, learning about projection methods, auxiliary views and section views. Lettering, tolerance, metric construction, technical sketching and orthographic projection, isometric drawing, oblique and perspective projection, fasteners, welds, and locking devices, training on allied trades viz. Hand Tools, Fitter, Turner, Machinist, Sheet Metal Worker, Welder, Foundry man, Electrician and Maintenance Motor Vehicles.

Workshop Calculation and Science include Unit, Fractions, Square Root, Ratio & Proportion, Ratio &Proportion, Material Science, Mass, Weight and Density, Speed and Velocity, Work, Power and Energy, Algebra, Mensuration, Trigonometry, Heat & Temperature, Basic Electricity, Levers and Simple Machines, Geometrical construction & theorem, Area of cut-out regular & irregular surfaces, Volume of cut-out solids, Material weight and cost, Forces definition, Thermal Conductivity, Average Velocity, Graph, Centre of gravity, Heat treatment, Concept of pressure and lots more.

We add new question answers with each new version. Please email us in case of any errors/omissions. This is arguably the largest and best e-Book for All engineering multiple choice questions and answers.

As a student you can use it for your exam prep. This e-Book is also useful for professors to refresh material.

Foreword

Vocational education and training is imparted through the Department of Vocational Education and Training through the Department of Business Education and Business Practical to supply multi-skilled artisans in line with the rapidly growing demand in the industrial sector in the 21st century. All the occupations within the institutions are important, as the trainees from these occupations develop multi-skills as per the demands of the industry.

with the noble intention of making available MCQ e-books suitable for all businesses, considering that all the examinations in all the industries in the industrial sector are conducted online and include MCQ method questions. Mr. Manoj Madhukar Dole has written a very good e-book on MCQ method as per the new annual syllabus. This e-book will definitely be a guide for all the trainees, trainee candidates, training instructors and others concerned.

The author of the book is Mr. Manoj Madhukar Dole, Instructor Gov. ITI Satara has 17 years of training experience. Written as a new annual pattern, this e-book incorporates modern digital QR Code technology to understand the layout, simple language, and simple syntax, diagrams and videos for each subject. So I am sure that this e-book will definitely be useful for in-depth study and exam practice. The work they have done is certainly commendable.

Mr. Tukaram Misal
Principal Government Industrial Training Institute Satara.

Preface

DGET New Delhi and CSTARI Kolkata have been implementing an annual pattern for all businesses in ITI since the August 2018 session. The examination system will also be changed and it will be online from this year and since all the questions are of Objective Type (MCQ), the trainees are in dire need of in-depth study. It is with this in mind that we are delighted to present the books based on the old NIMI pattern and a complete overview of the new annual pattern, and we hope that these books will be a guide for all business directors and trainees. Is.

For writing these books, Johar Awate Saheb, Principal of ITI Akluj. Former Principal of ITI Satara Saigavkar Saheb, Assistant Director Shri Chandrakant Dhekne Saheb Regional Office of Vocational Education and Training, Pune, District Vocational Education and Training Officer Sachin Dhumal Saheb and Headmaster Government Technical School Kendra Shalmali Pawar Madam and son Adhiraj Dole, mother Kusum Dole, I am very grateful to my father Madhukar Dole and wife Ashwini Dole for their special guidance and cooperation from time to time.

Also, in a very short period of time, the book was reviewed by Shri Rajendra Ghume Saheb, Joint Director, Vocational Education and Training Regional Office, Pune, for his invaluable time in publishing the book. I am sincerely grateful for their feedback.

I am grateful to the Instructor of ITI Satara for there continuous support from the very beginning of writing the book.

From this book, I consider myself blessed to have shared my thoughts on e-learning with you. I will not claim that this book is perfect, because considering the perfection, this book is an attempt and is in its infancy. They will be valuable for improvement if they are tested and suggested.

Manoj Dole
Dated 9/1/2019

Acknowledgements

The industrial training and theoretical examination system of our industrial training institutes and these changes have been accepted by the craft instructors and the trainees.

Theoretical examinations conducted in your industrial training institutes are also conducted online. Since these examinations are of multiple choice MCQ method, the trainees will need to get more practice of such questions.

With all these considerations in mind, Mr. Manoj Madhukar, Director, Dole Crafts, Katari Industrial Training Institute, Satara, has done a thorough study and with his diligent work and added his keen intellect, according to the new annual system and NSQF-5 syllabus, e-book of Katari and other machine trades. -Book) and they have created mobile apps and blogs on theoretical topics to make training easier and have made all these educational materials available for download on the world famous websites Google Play Store, Amazon and Apple Book Store. Training has been made easier by creating a print version and using advanced techniques like QR Code.

All these educational materials will definitely be a guide for all the trainees for in-depth study and for the craft instructors and other concerned who are imparting vocational training.

CHAPTER ONE

Engineering Drawing & Workshop Calculation and Science MCQ e- Learning

Online Test Exam
ITI Books
CNC Course
AutoCAD CAM
JOB & Apprentice
Online Theory
Computer Course
Trading Course
Web Designing
MSCIT Course
Shopping Business
Internet Business
Remotasks Course
Online Services
Top Sportsmans
Indian Army
Freedom Fighters
Top Scientists
Social Reformers
Motivational Speaker
Top Richest People
Join WhatsApp Group
Join Facebook Group
Like Facebook Page
PAN / Adhar / Licence Passport

Grinding

Fire extinguisher

French curve in drawing

Set square in drawing

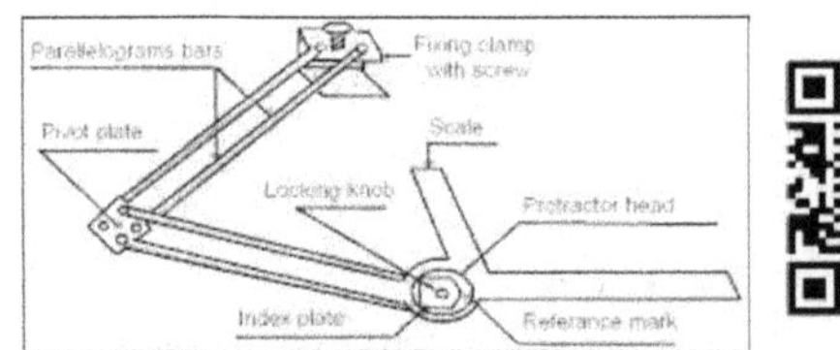

Mini drafter in drawing

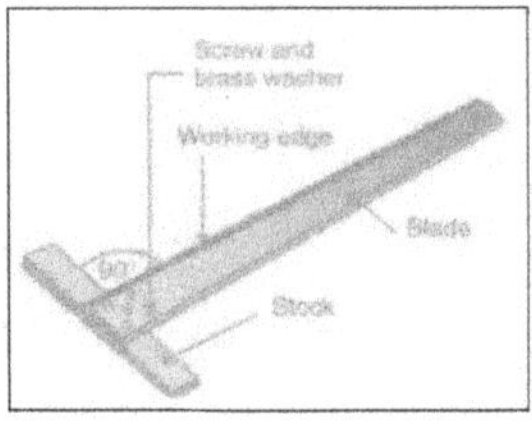

T - square in drawing

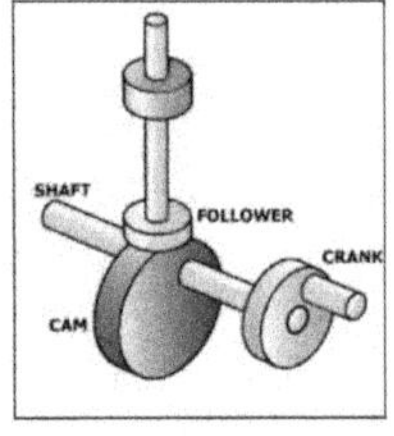

Cams in engine

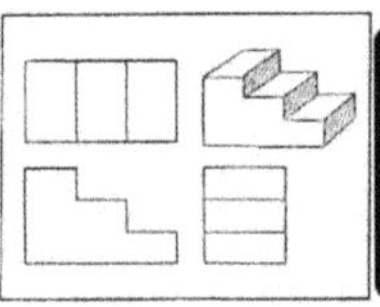

Orthographic projection in drawing

Third angle projection drawing

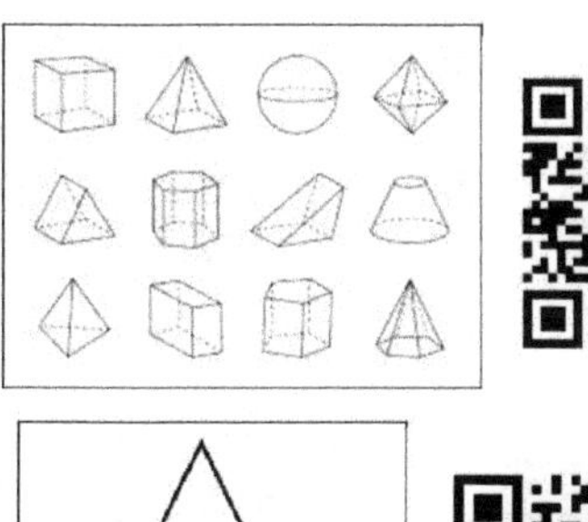

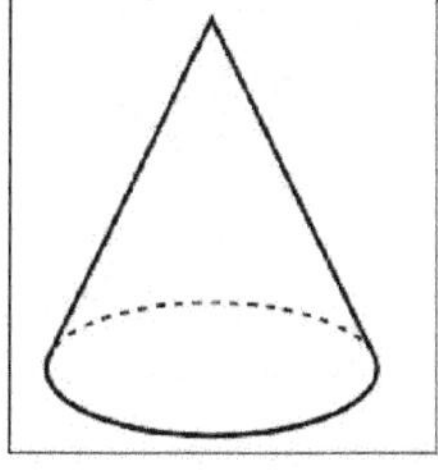

Cone in engineering drawing

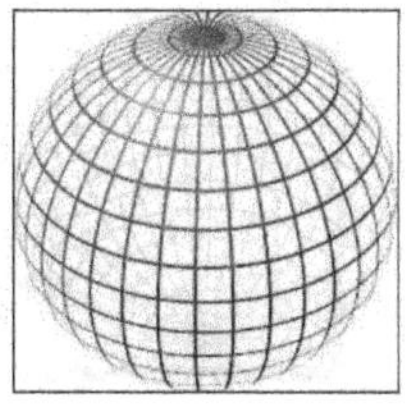

Sphere in drawing

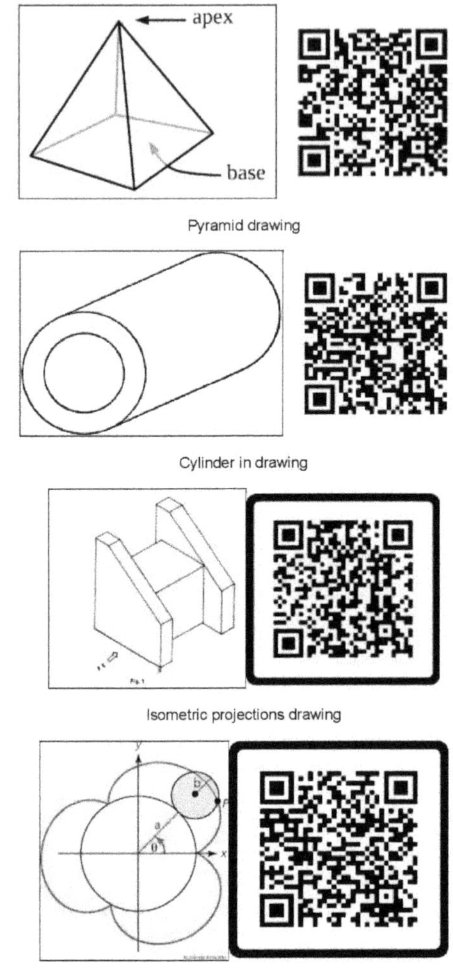

Pyramid drawing

Cylinder in drawing

Isometric projections drawing

Curves engineering drawing

Sectional views in drawing

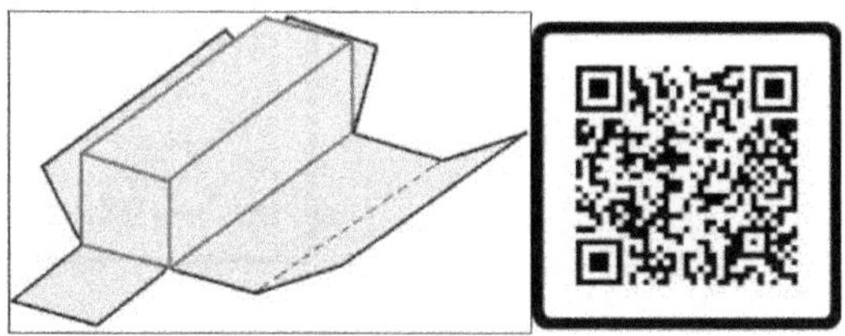

Development of surfaces in drawing

Hexagonal plane in drawing

Polyhedron in drawing

First Angle projection method in drawing

Springs in drawing

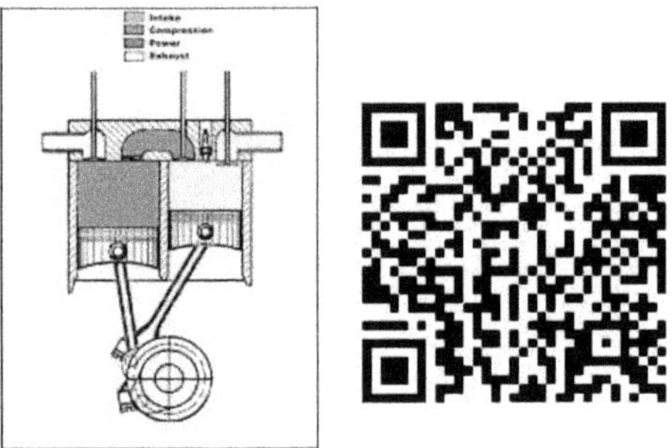

Engine in vehicle

Calliper

Hacksaw frame

Universal surface guage

Hammer

Centre punch

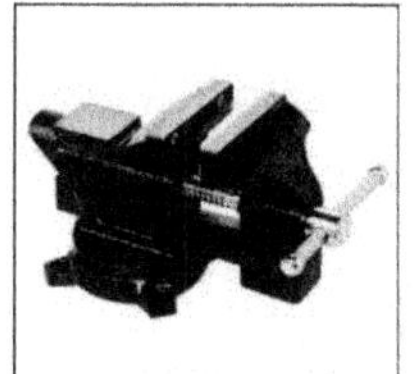

Bench vice

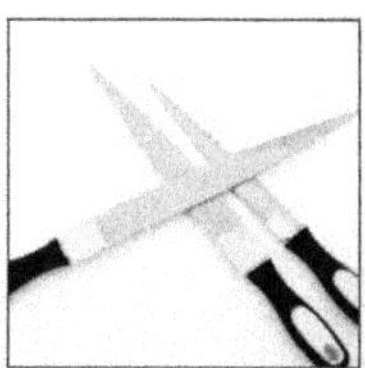

Files

Scraper

Workshop Calculation & Science

System of units Factors and Fractions

Square Root and Percentage

Material Science

Heat and Temperature and Pressure

Basic Electricity

Trigonometry

Friction

Centre of gravity

Area of cut out regular Surfaces and Irregular surfaces

Algebra

Elasticity

Heat Treatment

Profit and Loss

CHAPTER TWO

Engineering Drawing MCQ

1]The 'T' square is used for drawing lines ......

a] inclined

b] curved

c] vertical

d] horizontal

2] For drawing large size circle is drawn by.....

a] straight bar

b] lengthening bar

c] big bar

d] small bar

3] To draw or measure angle is used by.....

a]set square

b] protractor

c] 'T' square

d] none of these

4] The grade of pencil is used to sketching lettering ....

a] conical point

b] chisel point

c] soft

d] low

5] For drawing thin lines of uniform thickness the pencil should be sharpened in the form of ....

a] chisel edge

b]conical

c] pointed

d] none of these

23] What is used for drawing curves which can not drawn by compass

a] small compass

b] French curve

c] protractor

d] none of these

French curve in drawing

24]Unnecessary lines is removed by .....

a] Duster

b] sand paper block

c] eraser

d] none of these

25] Circle and arcs are drawn by means of .....l.

a] compass

b] divider

c] lengthening bar

d]none of these

26] Inking pen is used in drawing ......

a] horizontal line

b] non circular arcs

c] vertical lines

d] all of these

27] The card board scale are available in set of .....

a] 7

b] 8

c] 6

d] 9

28] The convenient length size of 30 -60°-90° set square for used in school and colleges are......

a] 250

b] 200

c] 300

d] none of these

Set square in drawing

29] Drawing board is shape of ....

a] square

b] rectangular
c] triangular
d] none of these
30] The 'T' square , set square ,scale protractor are complain use in.......
a] protractor
b] mini drafter
c] set square
d] none of these

Mini drafter in drawing

31]Set square , T square edges are bevelled for the purpose of....
a] curve line
b] inking lines
b] taking measurements
d] none of these

T - square in drawing

32]Geometrical construction which are mostly based on plane geometry and which are very.......

a] Accuracy

b] Quality

c] Essential

d] Superior quality

33] How much method of drawing the regular polygons.......

a] Inscribe circle method and arc method

b] General method for drawing any polygon

c] Alternative method

d] All of these

34] The line AB can be divided into .... equal parts.

a] 7

b] 10

c] 15

d] All of them

35] Which method of constructing triangl in circle......

a] Inscribing

b] Describing

c] Both a and b

d] None of these

36] When two sides of the hexagon are required to be horizontal the starting point for stepping equal division should be on an end of the.....

a] Horizontal diameter

b] Vertical diameter

c] Inclined diameter

d] None of these

37] If two sides of hexagon are required to be vertical the starting point should be on an end of the....

a] Inclined diameter

b] Horizontal diameter

c] Vertical diameter

d] None of these

38] The section obtained by the inter section of the right circular cone by a plane in different position relative to the axis of the cone are called.......

a] Conics

b] Circles

c] Triangles

d] Half circle

39] When the section plane is inclined to the axis and cuts all the generators on one side on a apex the section is in......

a] Conic section

b] Ellipse

c] Parabola

d] Hyperbola

40] When the section plane is inclined to the axis and is parallel to one of the generators the section is a ....

a] Ellipse

b] Parabola

c] Hyperbola

d] Cycloid

41] Use of elliptical curve is........

a] Arches

b] Dams and monuments

c] Manholes, gland & stuffing boxes

d] All of these

42] Use of parabolic curve is.........

a] Bridges & arches

b] Sound reflectors

c] Light reflectors

d] All of these

43] Use of hyperbolical curve is......

a] Cooling towers and water channel

b] Dames

c] Bridges

d] All of these

44] When the point is within the circle, the curve is called an.......

a] Superior trochoid

b] Interior trochoid

c] Trochoid

d] Isotrochoid

45] When the point outside the circle then the curve is called as......

a] Interior trochoid

b] Superior trochoid

c] Trochoid

d] Insuperior trochoid

46] The curve general by a point on a circumference of a circle, which rolls without slipping along another circle it is called.......

a] Epicycloids

b] Hypocycloid

c] Involute

d] None of these

47] When the circle rolls inside another circle the curve is called.......

a] Hypocycloid

b] Epicycloids

c] Trochoid

d] Hypotrochoid

48] The use of archemedian spiral curve is made in........

a] Teeth profiles of helical gears

b] Profiles of cams

c] Both a & b

d] None of these

Cams in engine

49] The cams are widely used in........

a] Automates

b] Printing machines

c] C engines

d] All of these

50] Spring index =

a] Diameter of coil / diameter of a wire

b] Diameter of wire /diameter of coil

c] Mean diameter of wire / diameter of coil

d] Mean diameter of a coil / diameter of wire

51] Eccentricity =

a] Distance of a point from the focus / distance of the point from directrix

b] Distance of focus from point / distance of point from

c] Distance of point from focus / distance of directrix of point

d] Distance of point from directrix / distance of point from focus

52] Mathematically an ellipse can be described by equation.....

a] $a^2 / X^2 + y^2 / b^2 = 1$

b] $x^2 / a^2 + y^2 / b^2$

c] $x^2 / a^2 + y^2 / b^2 = 0$

d] $x^2 / a^2 + y^2 / b^2 = 1$

53] Mathematically a parabola can be described by an equation......

a] $y^2 = 4ax$

b] $x^2 = 2ay$

c] $x^2 = 4ay$

d] Both a & b

54] Mathematically hyperbola can be described by an equation.......

a] $x^2 /a^2 - y^2 /b^2 = 1$

b] $x^2 /y^2 - y^2 /x^2 = 0$

c] Both a & b

d] None of these

55] Cycloid can be described by an equation......

a] y = a(1-cos Ø]

b] x = a(Ø -sin Ø]

c] Both a & b

d] None of these

56] The mathematically represented hypocycloid is.....

a] $Y = a \cos^3 Ø$, $X = a \sin^3 Ø$

b] $X = a \sin^3 Ø$, $Y = a \cos^3 Ø$

c] $X = a \cos^3 Ø$, $Y = a \sin^3 Ø$

d] None of these

57] Mathematically represented by involute is

a] X = r sin Ø - r Ø cos Ø, Y = r cos + r Ø sin Ø

b] X = r sin Ø + r cos Ø, Y = r cos Ø – r Ø sin Ø

c] Y = r Ø cos Ø – r sin Ø, X = r sin Ø – r Ø cos Ø

d] X = r cos Ø + r Ø sin Ø, Y =r sin Ø - r Ø cos Ø

58] The lines from the object to the plane are called.......

a] Projection

b] Projector

c] Reference plane

d] None of these

59] The orthographic projection an object is represented by View on the mutual perpendicular projection lines

a] Two or three

b] Three or two

c] Three or four

d] None of these

60] When the projectors are parallel to each other & also perpendicular to the plane, the projection is called......

a] Isometric projection

b] Oblique projection

c] Orthographic projection

d] Perspective projection

Orthographic projection in drawing

61] The two planes employed for the purpose of Orthographic projections are......

a] Auxillary plane

d] Horizontal plane

c] Reference plane

d] None of these

62] The line in which they intersect is termed the reference line & is denoted by the letters.......

a] AB

b] YZ

c] XY

d] None of these

63] The projection on the VP is called........

a] Side view

b] Front view

c] Top view

d] All of these

64] ....Method, when the views are drawn in their relative positions, the plane comes below the elevation. The view of the object as observed from the left-side the right of elevation.

a] Plane of projection

b] First angle projection

c] Third angle projection

d] None of these

65] Third angle projection method, the object is assumed to be situated in the........ quadrant.

a] First quadrant

b] Second quadrant

c] Third quadrant

d] Fourth quadrant

66] .... Method of projection is used in U.S.A & also in other countries.

a] plane of projection

b] Orthographic projection

c] First-angle projection

d] Third angle projection

Third angle projection drawing

67] When an object is situated on the ground, in first angle projection method, the bottom of its ..... will co-inside with XY

a] Top view

b] Front view

c] side view

d] All of these

68] The important element of this projection system

a] An object

b] Plane of projection

c] An observer

d] All of these

69] When line AB is parallel to HP hence ....

a] It' front view to AB

b] It''s side view equal to AB

c] It's top view equal to AB

d] None of these

70] When a line is parallel to a plane; it's projection on plane is equal to it's ;

a] True length

b] True shape

c] True size

d] None of these

71] The point is parallel in which the line or line produced meet the point is plane is called it's ....

a] Line

b] ratio

c] Trace
d] none of these
72] .... is the shortest distance between two points.
a] a line
b] a point
c] a straight line
d] none of these
73] When the line intersect horizontal plane that's called.....
a] horizontal trace
b] vertical trace
c] trace of line
d] none of these
74]Planes may be divided into two main types ......
a] Perpendicular planes, auxillary planes
b] Perpendicular plane, oblique planes
c] Auxillary planes , perpendicular planes
d] none of these
75] Planes which are inclined to the reference plane are called......
a] Auxillary plane
b] obliqeu plane
c] Perpendicular planes
d] picture plane
76] When a plane is perpendicular to a reference plane it's projection on that plane is a..........
a] horizontal line
b] parallel line
c] straight line
d] none of these
77] When a plane is parallel to a reference plane , it's projection on that plane shows........
a] It's true shape &size
b] It's true length & size
c] It's true height & size
d] none of these
78] Plane perpendicular to VP & HP that plane is called as ....
a] Auxillary Plane
b] Oblique Plane
c] Perpendicular Plane

d] None of these

79] Perpendicular plane can be divides into the following types.........

a] Perpendicular to both the reference planes.

b] Perpendicular to one plane & parallel to other

c] Perpendicular to one plane & inclined to other

d] <u>All of these</u>

80] The planes have only two dimensions, viz........

a] <u>Length & breadth</u>

b] Length & height

c] Length & thickness

d] All of these

81] The imaginary line of prism joining the centrs of the bases called.........

a] Faces

b] <u>Axis</u>

c] Apex

d] Base

82] A right & regular prism has it's axis....... to the bases

a] Parallel

b] <u>Perpendicular</u>

c] Inclined

d] None of these

83] When a pyramid or a cone is cut by a plane parallel to it's base thus removing the top portion, the remaining portion is called it's.........

a] Sphere

b] Cone

c] Cylinder

d] <u>Frustum</u>

Cone in engineering drawing

84] Oblique cylinder & cones have their axes........ to their base

a] Inclined

b] Parallel

c] Perpendicular

d] All of these

85] Projection of two equal sphere s resting on the ground & in contact with each other, with the line joining there centre parallel to the..........

a] A VP

b] VP

c] HP

d] All of these

Sphere in drawing

86] Projections of section on the other plane to which it is inclined is called.......

a] Section planes

b] Apparent section

c] True shape of sphere

d] None of these

87] When the section plane is parallel to the HP or the ground, the true shape of the section will be seen in.........

a] Front view

b] Side view

c] Top view

d] All of these

88] Surface of solid are laid out on a plane the figure obtained is called its........

a] Interpenetration

b] Development

c] Intersection

d] None of these

89] Development of surfaces is essential in.........

a] Foundry shop

b] Sheet metal work

c] Fitting shop

d] None of these

90] Which method of development used in transition pieces?

a] Parallel diameter

b] Radial line method

c] Triangulation method

d] Approximate method

91] Which method of development used in pyramids and cones.........

a] Radial line method

b] Parallel line method

c] Approximate method

d] Triangulation method

Pyramid drawing

92] Parallel line method is used in..........

a] Prism

b] Cylinder

c] Cubes

d] All of these

93] Which method of development used in surface as sphere, paraboloid, ellipsoid, hyperboloid, and helicoids

a] Radial line method

b] Triangulation method

c] Approximate method

d] Parallel line method

94] Zone method and lune method is used in development of........

a] Prisms

b] Cones

c] Sphere

d] Pyramids

95] Calculation the subtended angle Θ by the formula $\Theta = 360^0 \times$ radius of the base circle

a] Length of axis

b] Slant height

c] Radius of axis

d] None of these

96] In engineering practice, objects constructed may have constituent part, the surfaces of which intersect one another in lines called........ of intersection.

a] Lines

b] Cones

c] Cylinder

d] Prisms

97] The line of interaction may be depending upon the nature of.......

a] Intersection surface

b] Intersecting solids

c] Intersection cones

d] None of these

98] The two plane surface intersect in a........ line

a] Curve

b] Straight

c] Plane

d] All of these

99] The line of intersection between two curved surface or between......... Surface and a curved surface is a curve.

a] A curved

b] A plane

c] A solids

d] None of these

100] When a solids completely penetration another solids there will be two lines of intersection. These lines are sometimes called the line or........

a] Line of interpenetration

b] Curve of interpenetration

c] Solids of interpenetration

d] All of these

101] Use of penetration curve is.......

a] Sheet metal work

b] Fitting shop

c] Fabricating work

d] Foundry shop

102] Methods of determining the line of intersection between surface of two interpenetration.........

a] Approximate method & radial line method

b] Line method and cutting plane method

c] Triangulation method and parallel line method

d] None of these

103] Example of interpenetration is..........

a] Two prism intersection

b] Cylinder and prism intersection

c] Cone and cylinders intersection
d] All of these
104] Two cylinder intersection is example of.........
a] Intersection
b] Interpenetration
c] Cone intersection
d] None of these

Cylinder in drawing

105] .... Method is explained in detail while solving illustrative problems
a] Line method
b] Radial line method
c] Cutting plane method
d] Parallel line method
106] What is a type of isometric projection?
a] Pictorial projection
b] Orthographic projection
c] Perspective projection
d] Oblique Projection

Isometric projections drawing

107] Isometric views have been drawn........

a] Full scale

b] Half scale

c] True length

d] True scale

108] The line parallel to isometric axis are called........

a] Isometric axis

b] Isometric line

c] Isometric planes

d] Isometric views

109] The isometric projection is reduce in the ratio.........

a] 3 :

b] 1 : 2

c] 2 : 2

d] 2 : 3

110] The isometric projection of circle drawn with........

a] Isometric Plane

b] Isometric graph

c] Isometric Drawing

d] Isometric Scale

111] The major axis of the ellipse is long than...............

a] Radius of the circle

b] True diameter

c] Diameter of the circle

d] None of these

112] Makes practice for drawing of isometric view using........

a] Isometric planes

b] Isometric lines

c] Isometric graph

d] Isometric view

113] Use of parabolic curve is

a] Sound reflectors

b] Dams

c] Man hole of boiler

d] Gland & stuffing box

Curves engineering drawing

114] When the section plane is inclined the true shape of section on

a] AVP

b] VP

c] HP

d] A/P

115] When section plane is perpendicular to both the HP & VP the true shape of section on

a]Top view

b] Side view

c] Front view

d]None of this

116] When view projected on auxiliary planes are called

a] Auxiliary view

b Sectional view

c] Front view

d] None of these

117] Invisible features of an object are shown by means of

a] Outline

b] Chain lines

c] Hidden lines

d] None of these

118] Importance of sectional view on drawing for

a] Internal details

b] Outer details

c] Hatching

d] None of these

Sectional views in drawing

119] The component is cut by a straight cutting plane is divided in to two parts

a] Half section

b] Full section

c] Offset section

d] Removed section

120] section line is two different parts (pieces] in contact should be drown in...

a] Same direction

b] Opposite direction

c]parallel direction

d] None of these

121] When area to be sectioned in very small as for this plate and structural members blacked in section may be used. A space of not less than

a] 0.07mm

b] 0.7mm

c] 0.05mm

d] 0.5mm

122] The sum of interior angles of polygon is equal

a] (2*n-4]*Right angle

b] (2*n]*Right angle-4

c] (2*4-n]*Right angle

d] (2-4*n]*Right angle

123] One micron is equal to ....mm

a] 0.001

b] 1000

c] 0.01

d] 0.1

124] Development of surface is essential in.....

a] foundry shop

b] sheet metal work

c] fitting shop

d] none of these

Development of surfaces in drawing

125] Which method of development used in transition piece?

a] parallel line method

b] radial line method

c] triangulation method

d] none of these

126] The isometric projection is reduced in the ratio of

a] √2:√3

b] √3:√2

c] 1:√2

d] none of these

127] When measurements are required in three units the scale is used....

a] full scale
b] plain scale
c] half scale
d] none of these

128]Isometric drawing is larger in production about isometric projection is....

a] 22.5%
b] 0.815
c] 9/11
d] none of these

129] While isometric of sphere of spherical parts.......is must be used.

a] full scale
b] isometric length
c] true length
d] half scale

130] When circle draw with isometric scale the length of major axis of the ellipse to the ....

a] true diameter
b] isometric diameter
c] isometric diameter
d] none of these

131] In isometric view which contain a large number of non –isometric lines which method is used

a] box method
b] off-set method
c] co-ordinate method
d] centre lay out method

132] When drawing is drawn smaller than actual size of object .....

a] full scale
b] enlarging scale
c] reducing scale
d] none of these

133] When e=1 curve is called.....

a] parabola
b] hyperbola
c] ellipse
d] none of these

134]Compare with isometric drawing the advantage of oblique projection is....

a] front face is in true shape

b] two axis are always perpendicular to each othe

c] receding axis is taken at some convenient angles

d] none of these

135]If all the receding edges are drawn true length the oblique projection is called...

a] cavilier projection

b] cabinet projection

c] general projection

d] none of these

136] The large object such as building the point is usually taken height of .....

a] 0.8mm

b] 1.2mm

c] 1.8mm

d] 1.5mm

137] Central plane is the imaginary vertical plane which passes through....

a] P. P

b] H.L

c] G.P

d] C.P

138] When object is parallel to P.P the perspective is called......

a] one point

b] two point

c] three point

d] none of these

139] The line drawn through the station point from the picture plane shall be ....

a] P.A

b] H.L

c] G.L

d] C

140] The distance of the station point from the picture plane shall be .....

a] Max. Diameter of the object

b] Twice the max. Diameter of the object

c] Half the max. Diameter of the object

d] none of these

141] In isometric view of hexagonal plane all the sides of hexagon is .....

a] equal length

b] unequal length

c] none of these

Hexagonal plane in drawing

142] When all the faces are equal & regular the polyhedron is said....

a] regular

b] prisms

c] irregular

d] pyramid

Polyhedron in drawing

143] Oblique prisms & pyramid have ......

a] axis perpendicular to the base

b] axis inclined to the base

c] faces inclined to the H.P

d] none of these

144] Icosahedrons has equal equilateral triangular faces

a] 12

b] 8

c] 20

d] 6

145] When a pyramid or cone is cut by a plane parallel to its base is called.....

a] pyramid

b] turned carted

c] frustum

d] none of these

146] Plane which are inclined to both the reference plane is called ......

a] oblique plane

b] perpendicular plane

c] inclined plane

d] none of these

147] When a line parallel to H.P & perpendicular to V.P the trace line is.....

a] V.T

b] H.T

c] no trace

d] V.T& H.T

148] When a line parallel to the V.P and inclined to H.P the true length of line in.....

a] front view

b] top view

c] side view

d] none of these

149] When point situated in front quadrant

a] above the H.P & in front of V.P

b] below the H.P & in front of V.P

c] behind the V.P & above H.P

d] below the H.P & behind the V.P

150] Find the quadrant of point “b” is 15 mm above H.P and 25mm behind the V.P

a] I st

b] III rd

c] IIII th

d] II nd

151] In first angle projection front view is ......

a] above the top view

b] below the top view

c] above the side view

d] below the side view

First Angle projection method in drawing

152] In orthographic projection the projectors are ....

a] parallel to plane

b] perpendicular to plane

c] inclined to plane

d] none of these

153] L.H.S.V means.........

a] length of side view

b] left hand view

c] right hand view

d] left hand side view

154] The object lines between the observer and the plane of projection is ....

a] 3rd angle

b] 1st angle

c] 4th angle

d] 2nd angle

155] In third angle projection plane of projection is assumed to be ......

a] non transparent

b] quadrant

c] transparent

d] dihedral angle

156] In third angle projection top view is always on......

a] above front view
b] above top view
c] below the front view
d] below the side view
157] Four quadrants which may be called as......
a] anticlockwise
b] first and third angle
c] dihedral angles
d] none of these
158] In first angle projection method the view see from the left is placed on .....
a] left of the front view
b] right of front view
c] above the top view
d] below the front view
159] The size of A2 paper is .....
a] 297*420
b] 594*841
c] 420*594
d] 210*297
160] The edge of board on which 'T' square is sli9ding is called ......
a] straight edge
b] working edge
c] chisel edge
d] none of these
161] The size of title block as recommended by B.I.S . is .....
a] 185*65
b] 150*50
c] 170*65
d] none of these
169] The least count of a vernier calliper is ....
a] 0.001
b] 0.02
c] 0.001
d] 0.0002
170] Which scale is used to read a very small unit with great accuracy?
a] plain scale
b] diagonal scale

c] scale of chord

d] vernier scale

171] The R.F. is greater than one (1] the scale is ....

a] plain scale

b] diagonal scale

c] enlarging scale

d] reducing scale

172] The difference of one primary division and one vernier division is called......

a] least count

b] primary scale

c] vernier scale

d] R.F.

173] One micron is equal to in mm........

a] 1000mm

b] 0.001mm

c] 0.01mm

d] 100mm

174] the top surface joining the two sides of adjacent thread is called

A] Crest

B] Root

C] Flank

D] Thread is angle

175] The included angle of the ISO metric thread is --------

A] 27 1 /2°

B] 30°

C] 55°

D] 60°

176] Which one of the following screw thread forms has an included angle of 55° between the flanks of threads?

A] B. A. Thread

B] Acme thread

C] Buttress threads

D] Knuckle thread

177] Which one of the following is used only for finishing and maintaining correct form of thread?

A] Tap

B] Threading tool

C] Threading chaser

D] Tipped tool

Tap Die

178] The angle Of lS thread (V shaped] is ----------

A] 29°

B] 47 1/4°

C] 50°

D] 60

179] ln which of the following methods, only external threads are made -------

A] Form tool mEthOd

B] Compound rest method

C] Tailstock offset method

D] Taper turning attachment method.

180] The surface joining the crest and the root of a thread is known as ----

A] Flank

B] Shank

C] Pitch surface

D] All Of these

181] Pitch of a two start thread is 4 mm. Then the lead of the thread is given by -----

A] 4mm

B] 2mm

C] 8mm

D] 6mm

182] The Gear ratio required for cutting a screw thread of 2.5 mm on a lathe having a lead screw pitch using single point cutting tool is ----

A] 1:2

B] 2:1

C] 1:1 mm

183] The bottom surface joining the two sides of adjacent thread (external thread] is...

A] Flank

B] Root

C] Crest

D] Pitch

184] The form of thread used in carpenters vice is...

A] Square

B] Acme thread

C] Sawtooth Thread

D] Knuckle thread

185] What is the angle of pipe thread?

A] 60°

B] 47'/2°

C] 29°

D] 55°.

186] What is the use of pipe thread?

A] transmission

B] maintain pressure

C] airtight connections

D] none of the above.

187] What is the depth of the 2" pipe thread?

A] 0.5"

B] 0.640"

C] 0.335"

D] 0.580".

188] External Thread provide on Rod or Pipe , by Die and Cutting Tool is called ......

(A] Tapping

(B] Dieing

(C] Threading

(D] Grooving

189] Used where bolt and threads are to be protected from damage.

A] Donald cap nut

B] Thumb nut

C] Hexagonal nut

D] Wing-nut
190] Used where frequent removal and fixing is required.
A] Donald cap nut
B] Thumb nut
C] Hexagonal nut
D] Wing-nut
191] Used in machine building and structure work.
A] Donald cap nut
B] Thumb nut
C] Hexagonal nut
D] Wing-nut
192] Used where frequent adjustments are to be made.
A] Donald cap nut
B] Thumb nut
C] Hexagonal nut
D] Wing-nut
193] Nylon inserts in the nut prevent loosening.
A] Locking plate
B] Wire lock
C] Self-locking nut
D] Sawn nut
194] A slot is cut halfway across the nut.
A] Locking plate
B] Wire lock
C] Self-locking nut
D] Sawn nut
195] Prevents slackening of two bolts.
A] Locking plate
B] Wire lock
C] Self-locking nut
D] Sawn nut
196] Prevents rotation of the top nut.
A] Lock-nut
B] Grooved nut
C] Self-locking nut
D] Sawn nut
197] Prevents loosening of nut by the use of a plate shaped to fit the nut.
A] Locking plate

B] Wire lock

C] Self-locking nut

D] Sawn nut

198] Hexagonal nut with the lower part made cylindrical and the recessed groove.

A] Lock-nut

B] Grooved nut

C] Self-locking nut

D] Sawn nut

199] Filling up of the gap be» tween the bottom of the machine and the top of the floor or foundation block.

A] Wooden forms

B] Foundation bolts

C] Grouting

D] Template

200] Used to prevent any movement when the concrete is poured.

A] Wooden forms

B] Foundation bolts

C] Grouting

D] Template

201] Used to hold down the machine firmly on the foundation to prevent it from moving.

A] Wooden forms

B] Foundation bolts

C] Grouting

D] Template

202] Wooden patterns which represents the base of the machine and support bolts over the excavation.

A] Wooden forms

B] Foundation bolts

C] Grouting

D] Template

203] After placing this in the excavation it is firmly braced from the outside to withstand the pressure of concrete.

A] Wooden forms

B] Foundation bolts

C] Grouting

D] Template

204] Used to check the level of the machine

A] Crowbar

B] Spirit level

C] Levelling jacks

D] Wedge

210] For transmitting very low torque.

A] Feather key

B] Gib head key

C] Woodruff key

D] Saddle key

211] Profile of key tends to weaken the shaft.

A] Feather key

B] Gib head key

C] Woodruff key

D] Saddle key

212] For transmitting unidirectional torque.

A] Feather key

B] Gib head key

C] Woodruff key

D] Saddle key

213] For transmitting heavy torque.

A] Feather key

B] Gib head key

C] Woodruff key

D] Saddle key

214] For transmitting very high torque of the impact type in both directions of rotation.

A] Gib head key

B] Woodruff key

C] Saddle key

D] Tangential key

215] Permits sliding or axial movement of the mat« ing piece on the shaft.

A] Feather key

B] Gib head key

C] Woodruff key

D] Saddle key

216] Can be withdrawn easily.

A] Feather key
B] Gib head key
C] Woodruff key
D] Saddle key
237] Rivets for Joining sheets to thick plates.
A] Countersunk head
B] Flat head
C] Pan head
D] Mushroom
238] Rivets for Joining sheet metal.
A] Countersunk head
B] Flat head
C] Pan head
D] Mushroom
239] Rivets for Heavy fabrication work.
A] Countersunk head
B] Flat head
C] Pan head
D] Mushroom
240] Rivets for Reduces the height of rivet head above the meta\ surface
A] Countersunk head
B] Flat head
C] Pan head
D] Mushroom
241] Rivets for commonly used for structural work.
A] Countersunk head
B] Flat head
C] Pan head
D] Snap head
242] The caliper meant for measuring the width of a slot is...
A] Odd leg caliper
B] Outside caliper
C] Jenny caliper
D] Inside calliper

Calliper

243] The size of the dividers are specified by the -------

A] Total length of legs

B] Distance between the points when fully opened

C] Length of legs without points

D] distance between the pivot and the point

244] The instrument used to mark parallel lines, parallel to the datum edge is -

A] jenny caliper

B] Divider

C] Outside calliper

D] Inside calliper

245] Which one of the following is an indirect measuring tool?

A] Outside caliper

B] Vernier calliper

C] Steel rule

D] Outside micrometer

246] For cutting thin tubing, the most suitable pitch of the hacksaw blade is...

A] 1.8mm

B] 1.4mm

C] 1mm

D] 0.8mm

247] For cutting solid brass, the most suitable pitch of the hacksaw blade is...

A] 1.8mm

B] 1.4mm

C] 1mm

D] 0.8mm

248] A new hacksaw blade after a few strokes becomes loose because of the...

A] Stretching of the blade

B] Wing-nut threads being worn out

C] Wrong pitch of the blade

D] Improper selection of the set of saws.

Hacksaw frame

249] While cutting small diameter pipes, it is advisable to watch regularly and ensure that...

A] The cut is along the curved line

B] More saw teeth are in contract

C] The work is not overheated

D] Proper balancing of hacksaw is maintained

250] The vice clamps are used to...

A] Protect hard jaws

B] Clamp the work pieces rigidly

C] Protect the finished surfaces

D] Prevent the movable jaw being filed

251] The reference surface during marking is provided by the...

A] Surface gauge

B] Workpiece

C] Drawing of the work

D] Marking table surface

252] The size of an engineer's vice is specified by the...

A] Length of the movable jaw

B] Width of the jaws

C] Height of the vice

D] Maximum opening of the jaws

254] Scribers are made of...

A] Mild steel
B] High carbon steel
C] Brass
D] Cast iron
255] Portion of the hammer used for fixing the handle is...
A] Face
B] Peen
C] Cheek
D] Eye hole

Hammer

256] Weight of the hammer for the marking purpose is...
A] 250g
B] 500g
C] 1 kg
D] 2 kgs
257] The size of the dividers are specified by the...
A] Total length of the legs
B] Distance between the points when fully opened
C] Length of legs without the points
D] Distance between the pivot and the point
261] Name the punch used to locate the centre.
A] Prick punch 30°
B] Prick punch 60°
C] Centre punch
D] Dot punch
262] The point angle of centre punch is --------
A] 30°
B] 50°
c] 900

D] 1200

Centre punch

263] Punches are used for forming ---------of any shape

A] Holes

B] Mining

C] Knurling

D] Reaming

266] The convexity of files helps...

A] To file concave surfaces

B] To file convex surfaces

C] To prevent rounding of edges of work

D] The file to become straight when pressure is applied

267] Which file used for filling wood, leather and other soft material? .

A] Single cut file

B] Double cut file

c] Rasp cut file

D] Curved cut file

268] File used is used for ------------

A] Cleaning the work piece

C] Renewing the file teeth

B] cleaning the file teeth

D] Cleaning the chips

Files

269] File card is used to --------

A] Clean the work piece

C] Renew the file teeth

B] Clean the file teeth

270] The point angle of scriber is -----------

A] 30°

B] 60°

C] 5° to 10°

D] 12° to 15°

271] The cutting angle for chipping cast iron is...

A] 37.5°

B] 55°

C] 60°

D] 90°

272] The chisel will dig into the material when...

A] The rake angle is more

B] The clearance angle is too low

C] The angle of inclination is more

D] The angle of inclination is too low

CHAPTER THREE

Workshop Calculation & Science System of units Factors and Fractions MCQ

Scan for Theory Videos

1] What are the two classifications of system of units?
A] British and Metric
B] Gravitational and non-gravitational
C] Fundamental and derived
D] Metric and International
2] What are fundamental units?

A] Length, Mass, Volume
B] Length, Mass, Time
C] Length, Mass, Area
D] Length, Pressure, Volume
3] What denotes letter 'M' in MKS system?
A] Mile
B] Meter
C] Millimeter
D] Micron
4] How many millimetres are there in 1 inch?
A] 2.54 mm
B] 25.4 mm
C] 24.5 mm
D] 2.45 mm
5] What is the LCM of 12, 18, 6, 36?
A] 12
B] 18
C] 36
D] 42
6] What is the HCF of 18, 42, 24?
A] 2
B] 6
C] 18
D] 24
7] What is the improper fraction for the given mixed fraction ?
A] 52/7
B] 7/52
C] 28/7
D] 7/28
8] Convert decimal 0.000659 to fraction?
A] 659/1000
B] 659/10000
C] 659/100000
D] 659/1000000
9] Simplify = (3/4) +(2/5) -(5/20)
A] 3/10
B] 9/10
C] 12/10

D] 13/10

11] What is the product of 0.003 x 0.5? | 0.003 x 0.5

A] 0.00015

B] 0.0015

C] 0.015

D] 0.15

12] Simplify- (17.49 x 5.2) / 6.5

A] 13.69

B] 13.79

C] 13.89

D] 13.99

13] What is the length of each part if a copper wire of 225 metre long is cut into 900 equal parts?

A] 0.23 metre

B] 0.25 metre

C] 0.28 metre

D] 0.29 metre

CHAPTER FOUR

Square Root and Percentage MCQ

Scan for Theory Videos

14] What is the square root of 529?
A] 13
B] 23
C] 33
D] 43
15] What is the square of 0.01?
A] 0.001
B] 0.0001
C] 1.0E-5

D] 1.0E-6

16] What percentage of 80 is 20?

A] 80%

B] 40%

C] 25%

D] 20%

17] How much is 8% of 40 kg?

A] 2.2 kg

B] 3.2 kg

C] 4.2 kg

D] 5.2 kg

18] Convert 52% into fraction.

A] 9/25

B] 11/25

C] 13/25

D] 17/25

19] Convert 0.456 decimal fraction into percentage.

A] 45.6%

B] 4.56%

C] 0.456%

D] 0.0456%

20] What is the 'x' value for $x^2 + 6^2 = 10^2$?

A] 4

B] 6

C] 8

D] 10

21] What is the square root of decimal number 550.37?

A] 21.26

B] 22.26

C] 22.46

D] 23.46

22] What is the value of $\sqrt{8} + \sqrt{18} - 2\sqrt{2}$?

A] 2.24

B] 3.24

C] 4.24

D] 5.24

23] What is the side AB if AC = 10 cm and BC = 6 cm?

A] 8 cm

B] 6 cm

C] 5 cm

D] 4 cm

24] What is the side BC if AC = 15 cm and AB = 9 cm?

A] 4 cm

B] 8 cm

C] 10 cm

D] 12 cm

25] What is the value of side AC if AB = 7cm and BC = 5 cm?

A] 8.2 cm

B] 8.6 cm

C] 8.4 cm

D] 8.1 cm

26] What is the percentage of copper if the casting weight of copper 42.3 kg and tin weight 2.7 kg?

A] Cu 92%

B] Cu 94%

C] Cu 96%

D] Cu 98%

27] A motor cycle tyre is sold for Rs 300/- what is the purchase price if 25% profit is added to it.

A] Rs 200

B] Rs 220

C] Rs 240

D] Rs 260

28] What is the decimal fraction of conversion of 18.5%?

A] 0.185

B] 0.175

C] 0.165

D] 0.195

CHAPTER FIVE

Material Science MCQ

Scan for Theory Videos

29] Which one is non-metal?
A] Mercury | पारा
B] Graphite | ग्रेफाइ
C] Brass | पीतल
D] Iron | ल हा
30] Which metal contains iron as a major content?
A] Brass metal
B] Bronze metal
C] Zinc
D] Ferrous metal

31] What is the name of the metal which do not contain iron?

A] Ferrous metals

B] Non-ferrous metals

C] Insulating metals

D] Non-Insulating metals

32] Which one of the following is the mechanical properties of metal?

A] Fusibility

B] Ductility

C] Corrosion

D] Structure

33] Which is brittle metal?

A] Cast iron

B] Steel

C] Mild steel

D] Alloy steel

34] Which mechanical property of a metal offers resistance to elastic deformation in a cutting tool?

A] Ductility

B] Malleability

C] Hardness

D] Toughness

35] Which property of a metal is its ability to resist the effect of tensile forces?

A] Elasticity

B] Tenacity

C] Ductility

D] Brittleness

36] Which property of metal has its power of returning to its original shape after the applied force is released?

A] Malleability

B] Tenacity

C] Elasticity

D] Plasticity

37] Which property of a metal possessed by it melts when heat is applied?

A] Conductivity

B] Malleability

C] Fusibility

D] Tenacity
38] Which alloy used in electric lamp as filament?
A] Cobalt
B] Vanadium
C] Tungsten
D] Silicon
39] What metals contained in brass alloy?
A] Copper and aluminium
B] Copper and lead
C] Copper and zinc
D] Copper and tin
40] Which cast iron cannot be welded?
A] Grey cast iron
B] White cast iron
C] Malleable cast iron
D] Nodular cast iron
41] Which metal cannot be forged?
A] Alloy steel
B] Mild steel
C] Steel
D] Cast iron
42] Which metal is widely used for making casting of machinery parts?
A] Grey cast iron
B] White cast iron
C] Malleable cast iron
D] Wrought iron
43] Which furnace is used to get pig iron from iron ore?
A] Rever battery
B] Electric furnace
C] Blast furnace
D] Cupola
44] What is the name of furnace to obtained cast iron?
A] Cupola
B] Blast furnace
C] Rever battery
D] Electric furnace
45] What is the other name of low carbon steel?
A] Low alloy steel

B] High alloy steel
C] High speed steel
D] Mild steel
46] What is the carbon percentage in medium carbon steel?
A] 0.05% to 0.15%
B] 0.15% to 0.25%
C] 0.25% to 0.5%
D] 0.5% to 1.5%
47] What is the carbon percentage in low carbon steel?
A] 0.02% to 0.03%
B] 0.15% to 0.25%
C] 0.25% to 0.50%
D] 0.50% to 1.50%
48] What is the carbon percentage in high carbon steel?
A] 0.02% to 0.03%
B] 0.15% to 0.25%
C] 0.25% to 0.50%
D] 0.50% to 1.50%
49] What is the ore of aluminium?
A] Hematite
B] Mallatite
C] Bauxite
D] Lemonite
50] Which property of a metal enables it by which it can be drawn out into wires under tension without rupture?
A] Ductility
B] Malleability
C] Hardness
D] Brittleness
51] Which among the following is an insulator?
A] Copper
B] Aluminium
C] Silver
D] Mica
52] Which rubber is used as insulator for power cables and control wires?
A] Butyl
B] Hypalone

C] Silicon

D] Nitrite butadiene

53] Which alloy steel is used to make permanent magnets?

A] Silicon steel

B] Manganese steel

C] Vanadium steel

D] Cobalt steel

54] Which insulator is used in over head lines?

A] Mica

B] Rubber

C] P.V.C

D] Porcelain

55] Which insulating material is used for making switches?

A] Porcelain

B] PVC

C] Bakelite

D] Ebonite

56] What is the name of the property of an insulator that should brake down or puncture on application of high voltage?

A] Di-electric strength

B] Specific resistance

C] Mechanical strength

D] Non absorption

57] Which alloy steel is using for making precious instrument?

A] Silicon steel

B] Manganese steel

C] Invar steel

D] Vanadium

58] Which steel is used for making files and cold chisel?

A] Low carbon steel

B] Medium carbon steel

C] High carbon steel

D] Stainless steel

ANSWERS

1]C; 2]B; 3]B; 4]B; 5]C; 6]B; 7]A; 8]D; 9]B; 10]D; 11]B; 12]D; 13]B; 14]B; 15]B; 16]C; 17]B; 18]C; 19]A; 20]C; 21]D; 22]C; 23]A; 24]D; 25]B; 26]B; 27]C; 28]A; 29]B; 30]D; 31]B; 32]B; 33]A; 34]C; 35]B; 36]C; 37]C; 38]C; 39]C; 40]B; 41]D; 42]A; 43]C; 44]A; 45]D; 46]C; 47]B; 48]D; 49]C;

50]A; 51]D; 52]C; 53]D; 54]D; 55]C; 56]A; 57]C; 58]C;

CHAPTER SIX

Heat and Temperature and Pressure MCQ

Scan for Theory Videos

1] Which kind of heat transmission takes places by up-ward flow?

A] Conduction

B] Convection

C] Radiation

D] Reflection

2] Which one is the radiation method of heat transmission?

A] An iron rod is heated with one of its end and heat transmitted to other end

B] Cold water goes to the bottom from top while on heating the water

C] On heating gases, heat transmitted to surroundings

D] The heat from sun travels through the space

3] What is called if the length of the solid expands when heated?

A] Linear expansion

B] Superficial expansion

C] Cubical expansion

D] Area expansion

4] What is the change in length per unit original length per degree rise in temperature is called?

A] Co-efficient of friction

B] Co-efficient of linear expansion

C] Co-efficient of superficial expansion

D] Co-efficient of cubical expansion

5] What is the unit of co-efficient of linear expansion?

A] Number /°C

B] Number /°C / meter length

C] Number /°C / mm length

D] Number /°C / cm length

6] What is term used for 2 x linear expansion?

A] Co-efficient of friction

B] Co-efficient of linear expansion

C] Co-efficient of superficial expansion

D] Co-efficient of cubical expansion

7] What is term called for 3 x linear expansion?

A] Co-efficient of friction

B] Co-efficient of linear expansion

C] Co-efficient of superficial expansion

D] Co-efficient of cubical expansion

8] What is the co-efficient of linear expansion of a rod if it is found to be 100 m long at 20°C and 100.14 m long at 100°C?

A] 1.75×10^{-4}

B] 1.75×10^{-5}

C] 1.75×10^{-6}

D] 1.75×10^{-7}

9] What is called for the amount of heat required to raise the temperature of unit mass of a substance through 1°C?

A] Sensible heat

B] Latent heat

C] Specific heat
D] Mixing of heat

10] How much quantity of heat is required? m = 120 litres t1 = 20°C t2 = 85°C S = 4.2 Q = ______ KJ

A] 32750 KJ
B] 32760 KJ
C] 32770 KJ
D] 32780 KJ

11] Calculate the amount of heat required to raise the temperature of 85.5 gm of sand from 20°C to 35°C specific heat of sand = 0.1.

A] 128.25 Joules
B] 125.28 Joules
C] 128.26 Joules
D] 126.28 Joules

12] What is the specific heat of the material if we require 510 calories to raise the temperature of 170 gm of material from 50°C to 80°C?

A] 0.1
B] 0.01
C] 1.1
D] 1.11

13] How much quantity of heat is required to raise the temperature of 300 grams of copper (sp.heat 0.092 cal/gram) from 25°C to 75°C in Kcal?

A] 138 Kcal
B] 1.38 Kcal
C] 207 Kcal
D] 2.07 Kcal

14] How much heat is absorbed by a copper ingot weighing 400 Kg is heated from 30°C to 72°C for the purpose of forging? (sp.heat of copper is 0.09)

A] 1521 Kcal
B] 1251 Kcal
C] 1512 Kcal
D] 1215 Kcal

15] What is called for the materials that restricts heat flow by radiation, conduction and convection?

A] Conductors
B] Insulators
C] Ferrous

D] Non-ferrous

16] Which one is heat insulator?

A] Thermocole

B] Copper

C] Brass

D] Aluminium

17] Which one has the highest thermal conductivity?

A] Solid ice

B] Melting ice

C] Water

D] Steam

18] Which one of the following is not a property of heat insulating material?

A] Low conductivity

B] Resistance to fire

C] Less moisture absorption

D] Ductility

19] Which insulating material is most widely used in refrigerators?

A] Thermocole

B] Polyurethane

C] Glass wool

D] Cork sheet

20] Which one is a poor heat insulator?

A] Glass

B] Cork

C] Rubber

D] Saw dust

21] What is known for the temperature at which any solid melts into liquid?

A] Boiling point

B] Melting point

C] Latent heat of fusion

D] Latent heat of vaporisation

22] What is the melting point of aluminium?

A] 660°C

B] 680°C

C] 670°C

D] 620°C

23] What is the boiling point of aluminium?
A] 1897°C
B] 2519°C
C] 2469°C
D] 660°C
24] What is the boiling point of water?
A] 0°C
B] 32°C
C] 100°C
D] 212°C
25] What is the melting point of mercury?
A] -357°C
B] -209°C
C] -7.1°C
D] -38.72°C
26] What is the boiling point of mercury?
A] 357°C
B] 280°C
C] 759°C
D] 767°C

CHAPTER SEVEN

Basic Electricity MCQ

Scan for Theory Videos

27] Which machine converts mechanical energy into electrical energy?

A] Battery

B] Generator

C] Heater

D] Iron box

28] Which is the unit of current?

A] Ampere

B] Volt

C] Ohm

D] Watt

29] Which is the unit of resistance?

A] Ampere
B] Volt
C] Ohm
D] Watt

30] What is the flow of electrons in any conductor?
A] Voltage
B] Current
C] Resistance
D] Power

31] Which property of a substance is opposing the flow of electric current?
A] Current
B] Voltage
C] Resistance
D] EMF

32] Which is very good conductor?
A] Copper
B] Cast iron
C] Wrought iron
D] Steel

33] Which is mineral insulator?
A] Glass
B] Quartz
C] Mica
D] Porcelain

34] What is the total resistance if three resistances of 3 ohms, 9 ohms and 5 ohms are connected in series?
A] 11 ohms
B] 7 ohm
C] 17 ohms
D] 1/17 ohms

35] What is the total resistance if two resistances of 4 ohms and 6 ohms are connected in parallel?
A] 2.4/10
B] 24/10
C] 10/24
D] 10/2.4

36] What is the total resistance if three resistances of 4 ohms, 6 ohms and 8 ohms respectively are connected in parallel?

A] 24

B] 13

C] 24/13

D] 13/24

37] Which is same in series connection of resistors in a circuit?

A] Current

B] Voltage

C] Resistance

D] Power

38] Which law states that at constant temperature the current passing through a closed circuit is directly proportional to the potential difference and inversely proportional to the resistance?

A] Ohm's law

B] Lenz's law

C] Newton's law

D] Hooke's law

39] What is the resistance? I = 11.5 Amps V = 380 Volts R = ________Ohms

A] 13 ohms

B] 23 ohms

C] 33 ohms

D] 43 ohms

40] What is the current? R = 50 Ohms 220 Volts I =________Amps

A] 4.1 Amps

B] 4.2 Amps

C] 4.3 Amps

D] 4.4 Amps

41] What is the voltage? R = 250 Ohms I = 0.44 Amps V = ______Volts

A] 100 Volts

B] 105 Volts

C] 108 Volts

D] 110 Volts

42] Which statement is correct according to ohm's law?

A] I µ 1/V

B] I µ R

C] I μ V/R

D] I μ R/V

43] What is the filament resistance if a 6 volt bulb draws a current of 0.5 Amps?

A] 12 Ω

B] 10 Ω

C] 3 Ω

D] 1.2 Ω

44] How much watt second in 1 watt hour?

A] 1000 watt sec

B] 2000 watt sec

C] 3600 watt sec

D] 4000 watt sec

45] What is the power if an emf of one volt causes a current flow of 1ampere?

A] 1 watt

B] 1 kilowatt

C] 1 HP

D] 1 Kilowatt hour

46] Which is equal to electric power?

A] R^2 I watts

B] I^2 R watts

C] R^2 / I watts

D] I^2 / R watts

47] How much power does it consumes if an electric heater draws a current of 10 amps at 200 volts?

A] 2000 watts

B] 2010 watts

C] 2020 watts

D] 2030 watts

48] What is the resistance of an electric iron if the rating of electric iron is 220 V and 500 watts?

A] 94.8 ohms

B] 95.8 ohms

C] 96.8 ohms

D] 97.8 ohms

49] What is the voltage of the immersion heater? P = 500 watts I = 2.27 Amps V = ______Volts

A] 200.3 volts

B] 210.3 volts

C] 220.3 volts

D] 230.3 volts

50] Which is the unit electrical power?

A] Volts

B] Ohms

C] Watts

D] Ampere

51] What is the current Flow in the bulb? P = 550 watts R = 22 Ohms I = ______Amps

A] 2 Amps

B] 3 Amps

C] 4 Amps

D] 5 Amps

52] What is the power required? I = 0.455 Amps R = 484 Ohms P = _____Watts

A] 98.2 watts

B] 99.2 watts

C] 100.2 watts

D] 101.2 watts

53] What is the rated power if an adjustable resistor bears the following label 1.5 k ohms/ 0.08A?

A] 9.2 watts

B] 9.4 watts

C] 9.6 watts

D] 9.8 watts

54] How much voltage will be required to illuminate a 40 watts fluorescent lamp draws a current of 0.10 amperes?

A] 390 volts

B] 395 volts

C] 400 volts

D] 405 volts

55] How many hours will take for a 100 watts bulb to consume 1 kwh energy? W = 1 Kwh P = 100 Watts t = _____Hours

A] 10 hours

B] 12 hours
C] 18 hours
D] 24 hours

CHAPTER EIGHT

Trigonometry MCQ

Scan for Theory Videos

56] How many degrees is equal to one radian?

A] $\pi°/360$

B] $360°/\pi$

C] $\pi°/180$

D] $180°/\pi$

57] Which is equal to $\sin\theta$?

A] Opposite side / Hypotenuse

B] Hypotenuse / Opposite side

C] Adjacent side / Hypotenuse

D] Hypotenuse / Adjacent side

58] What is equal to cosθ?
A] Hypotenuse / Adjacent side
B] Adjacent side / Hypotenuse
C] Opposite side / Hypotenuse
D] Hypotenuse / Opposite side
59] What is equal to tanθ?
A] Opposite side / Hypotenuse
B] Adjacent side / Hypotenuse
C] Opposite side / Adjacent side
D] Adjacent side / Opposite side
60] What is the value of tanθ if sinθ = 4/5?
A] 4/5
B] 5/3
C] 3/4
D] 4/3
61] What is the value of θ if sinθ = √3/2 ?
A] 30°
B] 45°
C] 60°
D] 90°
62] What is the value of tan 45° if sin 45° = 1/√2 ?
A] 1/√2
B] √3/2
C] 1
D] 1/√3
63] What is the value of sin 30° if cos 30° = √3/2 ?
A] √3/2
B] 1/2
C] 1/√3
D] 1/√2
64] What is 1 + $\cot^2\theta$?
A] sec^2q
B] $cosec^2q$
C] cot^2q
D] tan^2q
ANSWERS

1]B; 2]D; 3]A; 4]B; 5]A; 6]C; 7]D; 8]B; 9]C; 10]B; 11]A; 12]A; 13]B; 14]C; 15]B; 16]A; 17]A; 18]D; 19]B; 20]A; 21]B; 22]A; 23]B; 24]C; 25]D; 26]A; 27]B; 28]A; 29]C; 30]B; 31]C; 32]A; 33]C; 34]C ; 35]B; 36]C; 37]A; 38]A; 39]C; 40]D; 41]D; 42]C; 43]A; 44]C; 45]A; 46]B; 47]A; 48]C ; 49]C; 50]C; 51]D; 52]C; 53]C; 54]C; 55]A; 56]D; 57]A; 58]B; 59]C; 60]D; 61]C; 62]C; 63]B; 64]B;

1] What are the two classifications of system of units?

A] British and Metric

B] Gravitational and non-gravitational

C] Fundamental and derived

D] Metric and International

2] What are fundamental units?

A] Length, Mass, Volume

B] Length, Mass, Time

C] Length, Mass, Area

D] Length, Pressure, Volume

3] What denotes letter M in MKS system?

A] Mile

B] Meter

C] Millimeter

D] Micron

4] How many millimetres are there in 1 inch?

A] 2.54 mm

B] 25.4 mm

C] 24.5 mm

D] 2.45 mm

5] What is the LCM of 12, 18, 6, 36?

A] 12

B] 18

C] 36

D] 42

6] What is the HCF of 18, 42, 24?

A] 2

B] 6

C] 18

D] 24

11] What is the product of 0.003 x 0.5?

A] 0.00015

B] 0.0015

C] 0.015

D] 0.15

13] What is the length of each part is a copper wire of 225 metre long is cut into 900 equal parts?

A] 0.23 metre

B] 0.25 metre

C] 0.28 metre

D] 0.29 metre

14] What is the square root of 529?

A] 13

B] 23

C] 33

D] 43

15] What is the square root of 0.017?

A] 0.001

B] 0.13

C] 0.00001

D] 0.000001

16] What is the definition of ratio?

A] Relation of two quantities of the same kind

B] Relation of two quantities of the different kind

C] Equality between two ratios

D] Inequality between two ratios

17] What is the ratio of 4 kg to 800 grams?

A] 5] 1

B] 4] 8

C] 8] 4

D] 2] 4

18] What percentage of 80 is 20?

A] 0.8

B] 0.4

C] 0.25

D] 0.2

19] How much is 8% of 40 kg?

A] 2.2 kg

B] 3.2 kg

C] 4.2 kg

D] 5.2 kg

21] Convert 0.456 decimal fraction into percentage?

A] 45.6%

B] 0.0456 %

C] 0.456%

D] 0.0456%

22] What is the x value for x2 + 62 = 102?

A] 4

B] 6

C] 8

D] 10

23] What is the square root of decimal number 550.37?

A] 21.26

B] 22.26

C] 22.46

D] 23.46

24] What is the value of Ö8 + Ö18 - 2Ö2?

A] 2.24

B] 3.24

C] 4.24

D] 5.24

25] What is the side AB if AC = 10 cm and BC = 6 cm?

A] 8 cm

B] 6 cm

C] 5 cm

D] 4 cm

26] What is the side AB, if BC = 15 cm and AC = 9 cm?

A] 4 cm

B] 8 cm

C] 10 cm

D] 12 cm

27] What is the value of side AC if AB = 7 cm and BC = 5 cm?

A] 8.2 cm

B] 8.6 cm

C] 8.4 cm

D] 8.1 cm

28] What is the length L2, if total length (L) is 2.75 metre and L1] L2 = 2] 3?

A] 1.1 metre
B] 1.25 metre
C] 1.65 metre
D] 1.75 metre

29] How many days a mechanic takes to assemble 64 machines if he assembles 8 machines in 3 days?

A] 20 days
B] 22 days
C] 24 days
D] 26 days

30] What will be the rpm of smaller gear if a 180 mm dia meshes with 60 mm dia gear and the bigger gear makes 60 rpm?

A] 120 rpm
B] 140 rpm
C] 160 rpm
D] 180 rpm

31] What is the percentage of copper if the casting weight of copper 42.3 kg and tin weight 2.7 kg?

A] Cu 92%
B] Cu 94%
C] Cu 96%
D] Cu 98%

32] A motor cycle tyre is sold for Rs 300/- what is the purchase price if 25% profit is added to it.

A] Rs 200
B] Rs 220
C] Rs 240
D] Rs 260

33] What is the decimal fraction of conversion of 18.5%?

A] 0.185
B] 0.175
C] 0.165
D] 0.195

34] Which one is non-metal?

A] Mercury
B] Graphite
C] Brass
D] Iron

35] Which metal contains iron as a major content?

A] Brass metal

B] Bronze metal

C] Zinc

D] Ferrous metal

36] What is the name of the metal which do not contain iron?

A] Ferrous metals

B] Non-ferrous metals

C] Insulating metals

D] Non-Insulating metals

37] Which one of the following properties is the mechanical properties of metal?

A] Fusibility

B] Ductility

C] Corrosion

D] Structure

38] Which is brittle metal?

A] Cast iron

B] Steel

C] Mild steel

D] Alloy steel

39] Which mechanical property of a metal offers resistance to elastic deformation in a cutting tool? A] Ductility

B] Malleability

C] Hardness

D] Toughness

40] Which property of material enables to formation of permanent deformation without fracture?

A] Elasticity

B] Plasticity

C] Ductility

D] Brittleness

41] Which property of metal has its power of returning to its original shape after the applied force is released?

A] Malleability

B] Tenacity

C] Elasticity

D] Plasticity

42] Which property of a metal possessed by it melts when heat is applied?

A] Conductivity

B] Malleability

C] Fusibility

D] Tenacity

43] Which alloy used in electric lamp as filament?

A] Cobalt

B] Vanadium

C] Tungsten

D] Silicon

44] What metals contained in brass alloy?

A] Copper and aluminium

B] Copper and lead

C] Copper and zinc

D] Copper and tin

45] Which cast iron cannot be welded?

A] Grey cast iron

B] White cast iron

C] Malleable cast iron

D] Nodular cast iron

46] Which metal cannot be forged?

A] Alloy steel

B] Mild steel

C] Steel

D] Cast iron

47] Which metal is widely used for making casting of machinery parts?

A] Grey cast iron

B] White cast iron

C] Malleable cast iron

D] Wrought iron

48] Which furnace is used to get pig iron from iron ore?

A] Mild steel - Rever battery

B] Electric furnace

C] Blast furnace

D] Cupola

49] What is the name of furnace to obtained cast iron?

A] Cupola

B] Mild steel - Blast furnace
C] Steel - Rever battery
D] Alloy metal - Electric furnace
50] What is the other name of low carbon steel?
A] Low alloy steel
B] High alloy steel
C] High speed steel
D] Mild steel
51] What is the carbon percentage in medium carbon steel?
A] 0.05% to 0.15%
B] 0.15% to 0.25%
C] 0.25% to 0.5%
D] 0.5% to 1.5%
52] What is the carbon percentage in low carbon steel?
A] 0.02% to 0.03%
B] 0.15% to 0.25%
C] 0.25% to 0.50%
D] 0.50% to 1.50%
53] What is the carbon percentage in high carbon steel?
A] 0.02% to 0.03%
B] 0.15% to 0.25%
C] 0.25% to 0.50%
D] 0.50% to 1.50%
54] What is the ore of aluminium?
A] Hematite
B] Mallatite
C] Bauxite
D] Lemonite
55] Which property of a metal enables it by which it can be drawn out into wires under tension without rupture?
A] Ductility
B] Malleability
C] Hardness
D] Brittleness
56] Which among the following is an insulator?
A] Copper
B] Aluminium
C] Silver

D] Mica

57] Which rubber is used as insulator for power cables and control wires?

A] Butyl

B] Hypalone

C] Silicon

D] Nitrite butadiene

58] Which alloy steel is used to make permanent magnets?

A] Silicon steel

B] Manganese steel

C] Vanadium steel

D] Cobalt steel

59] Which insulator is used in over head lines?

A] Mica

B] Rubber

C] P.V.C

D] Porcelain

60] Which insulating material is used for making switches?

A] Porcelain

B] PVC

C] Bakelite

D] Ebonite

61] What is the name of the property of an insulation that should brake down or puncture on application of high voltage?

A] Di-electric strength

B] Specific resistance

C] Mechanical strenth

D] Non absorption

62] Which alloy steel is using for making precious instrument?

A] Silicon steel

B] Manganese steel

C] Invar steel

D] Vanadium

63] Which steel is used for making files and cold chisel?

A] Low carbon steel

B] Midium carbon steel

C] High carbon steel

D] Stainless steel

64] What is termed as the quantity of matter contained in a body?

A] Density

B] Volume

C] Mass

D] Specific gravity

65] What is the force with which a body is attracted by the earth towards its centre?

A] Mass

B] Weight

C] Volume

D] Density

66] What is called mass per unit volume of a substances?

A] Mass

B] Weight

C] Density

D] Volume

67] What is called the ratio between the density of a substances density of water at 4°C?

A] Density

B] Specific gravity

C] Mass

D] Weight

68] What is the density of aluminium?

A] 2.7 g/cm3

B] 3.7 g/cm3

C] 4.7 g/cm3

D] 5.7 g/cm3

69] Wha is the mass if the density of a body is 7.6 g/cm3 and its volume is 25 cm3?

A] 190 grams

B] 200 grams

C] 210 grams

D] 220 grams

70] What is the specific gravity of the solid, if density of the solid is 19.5 g/cm3?

A] 18.0

B] 18.5

C] 19.0

D] 19.5

71] What is the density (r) in g/cm3 of an iron cube, if it weighs (W) 4.8 kg and volume (V) is 640 cm3?

A] 6.6 g/cm3

B] 6.9 g/cm3

C] 7.2 g/cm3

D] 7.5 g/cm3

72] What is the volume (V) of mercury in cm3, if mass (m) of mercury is 1 kg and density (r) is 13.6 g/cm3?

A] 73.53 cm3

B] 73.43 cm3

C] 73.33 cm3

D] 73.23 cm3

73] What is the mass in gram, if a force of 15 dyres acting on a mass m producing an acceleration of 2.5 cm/sec2?

A] 9 grams

B] 8 grams

C] 7 grams

D] 6 grams

74] What is the specific gravity of the metal, if the piece of metal weighs 150 grams in air and 125 grams in water?

A] 6

B] 10

C] 15

D] 25

75] What is the volume of mercury in cm3, if the mass (m) of mercury is 136 grams (g) and density (r) of mercury is 13.6 g/cm3?

A] 136 cm3

B] 13.6 cm3

C] 10.6 cm3

D] 10.0 cm3

76] What is the block weighs (W) in kg, if volume (V) is 320 cm3 and density 8.9 g/cm3?

A] 2.948 kg

B] 2.848 kg

C] 2.648 kg

D] 2.448 kg

77] What is the specific gravity of the metal, if the weighs 6.5 kgf in air and 3.5 kgf in water?

A] 6.166

B] 3.166

C] 2.166

D] 1.166

78] What is the weight force of a car has a mass of 800 kg?(Take g = 9.81m/sec)

A] 7848 Newton

B] 7748 Newton

C] 7847 Newton

D] 7487 Newton

79] What is the formula for speed?

A] Distance covered/Time

B] Change in velocity/Time

C] Distance in definite direction /Time

D] Change in momentum/Time

80] What is the unit of speed?

A] Metre/second

B] Metre/second2

C] Metre/minute

D] Metre/hour

81] What is the formula for velocity?

A] Distance covered/Time

B] Displacement/Time

C] Change in velocity/Time

D] Change of momentum/Time

82] What is the unit for velocity?

A] Metre/second

B] Metre/second2

C] Metre/minute

D] Metre/hour

83] What is called if a body posses only magnitude or size alone?

A] Speed

B] Velocity

C] Vector quantity

D] Scalar quantity

84] What is called if a body posses both magnitude and direction of velocity?

A] Speed

B] Velocity

C] Vector quantity

D] Scalar quantity

85] What is the rate of change of displacement of a body?

A] Body at rest

B] Body at motion

C] Speed

D] Velocity

86] What is called if a body does not change its position with respect to its surroundings?

A] Body at motion

B] Body at rest

C] Speed

D] Velocity

87] What is called if a body changes its position with respect to its surroundings?

A] Body at rest

B] Body at motion

C] Speed

D] Velocity

88] What is velocity of a body travels a distance of 168 metres in a line in 21 seconds?

A] 6 m/sec

B] 8 m/sec

C] 10 m/sec

D] 12 m/sec

89] What is the speed of a train of 80 metre long train passes a railway station platform of 120 metres length in 20 seconds?

A] 30 km/hour

B] 32 km/hour

C] 34 km/hour

D] 36 km/hour

91] What is the unit of acceleration of an object?

A] Metre/second

B] Metre/second2

C] Metre/minutes

D] Metre/minutes2

92] What is the acceleration of a car if the speed of the car has increased from 25 km per hour to 40 km per hour in one minute?

A] 0.059 m/sec2

B] 0.59 m/sec2

C] 0.069 m/sec2

D] 0.69 m/sec2

93] What is the retardation of a car moving with a velocity of 50 km/hr is brought to rest in 45 seconds?

A] 0.40 m/sec2

B] 0.30 m/sec2

C] 0.20 m/sec2

D] 0.10 m/sec2

94] What is the acceleration of an aeroplane taking off from landing field has to run 700 metres if it leaves the ground in 10 seconds from the start?

A] 8 metre/sec2

B] 10 metre/sec2

C] 12 metre/sec2

D] 14 metre/sec2

95] What maximum height a stone will reach if it is thrown upwords with a velocity of 20m/sec?(g = 10m/sec2)

A] 10 m

B] 20 m

C] 30 m

D] 40 m

96] What is the work done in unit time?

A] Energy

B] Power

C] Force

D] Acceleration

97] What is the capacity of a body to do work is called?

A] Energy

B] Power

C] Acceleration

D] Force

98] What is the ratio of power output to power input?

A] Work
B] Energy
C] Efficiency
D] Acceleration

99] What is called if a force of 1Newton acts on a body and moves it through a distance of 1 metre? A] 1 Joule
B] 10 Joules
C] 1 dyne
D] 10 dynes

100] How many ergs for 1 Joule?
A] 103 ergs
B] 105 ergs
C] 107 ergs
D] 109 ergs

101] How many newtons for 1 kilogram?
A] 981 Newtons
B] 98.1 Newtons
C] 9.81 Newtons
D] 0.981 Newtons

102] How many watts for 1 horse power in metric system?
A] 725.5 watts
B] 735.5 watts
C] 745.5 watts
D] 755.5 watts

103] How many watts for 1 horse power in British system?
A] 726 watts
B] 736 watts
C] 746 watts
D] 756 watts

104] What is the equivalent unit for 1horse power in metric system?
A] 75 kg.m/sec
B] 76 kg.m/sec
C] 77 kg.m/sec
D] 78 kg.m/sec

105] What is the formula for potential energy?
A] mgh joule
B] mgh2 joule
C] 1/2 mgh joule

D] 2/3 mgh joule

106] What is the formula for kinetic energy?

A] 1/2 mv joule

B] 1/2 mv2 joule

C] 2/3 mv2 joule

D] 2/3 mv joule

107] How much work done in one hour, if a pump can raise 100 liters of water through a height of 200 meters in one minutes?

A] 12 x 104 kg meter

B] 12 x 105 kg meter

C] 12 x 106 kg meter

D] 12 x 107 kg meter

108] What is the work done, if a force of 250 newtons acted upon a body and the body has been moved through a distance of 15 metres?

A] 3720 Joules

B] 3730 Joules

C] 3740 Joules

D] 3750 Joules

109] What is the potential energy, if a body of mass 250 kg is at a height of 30 metre?

A] 72.57 KJ | 72.57 KJ

B] 73.57 KJ | 73.57 KJ

C] 74.57 KJ | 74.57 KJ

D] 75.57 KJ | 75.57 KJ

110] What is the potential energy in a body of mass 10 kg kept on the top of a pole 20 metres height?

A] 1942 Joules

B] 1952 Joules

C] 1962 Joules

D] 1972 Joules

111] What is the work done in joules if a load of 15.5 kg is lifted through a height of 4.4 metres?

A] 639 Joules

B] 649 Joules

C] 659 Joules

D] 669 Joules

112] What is the kinetic energy of a bullet of mass 5gm travels with a speed of 500 m/sec?

A] 620 Joules
B] 625 Joules
C] 630 Joules
D] 635 Joules
113] Which refers the temperature?
A] It is a form of energy
B] It tells the state of heat
C] It tells specifie heat of substance
D] It is measured by calorie meter
114] What is the S.I unit of heat?
A] Calorie
B] Joule
C] Centigrade heat unit
D] British thermal unit
115] Which instrument is used to measure heat?
A] Calorie meter
B] Thermometer
C] Pyrometer
D] Barometer
116] What is the quantity of heat required to raise the temperature of 1 gram of water through 1°C is called?
A] Specific heat
B] Colorie
C] British thermal unit
D] Centigrade heat unit
117] What is the value for specific heat of water?
A] 4
B] 3
C] 2
D] 1
118] Which type heat is the heat absorbed or given off by a substance without changing its physical state?
A] Latent heat
B] Sensible heat
C] Specific heat
D] Latent heat of steam
119] What is the boiling point of water in fahrenheit scale?
A] 212°F

B] 180°F
C] 112°F
D] 100°F

120] What is the freezing point of water in kelvin scale (K)?
A] 373°K
B] 313°K
C] 303°K
D] 273°K

121] Convert 45°C (Centigrade) into °F (Fahrenheit).
A] 110°F
B] 111°F
C] 112°F
D] 113°F

122] At what temperature will Fahrenheit and centigrade thermometers give the same reading?
A] -38°C
B] -39°C
C] -40°C
D] -41°C

123] Convert - 273°C (Centigrade) into kelvin scale?
A] 0°K
B] 1°K
C] 2°K
D] 3°K

124] What is the value in degree centigrade for 20°F?
A] -6.37°C
B] -6.47°C
C] -6.57°C
D] -6.67°C

125] What is the maximum temperature that can be measured by mercury thermometer?
A] 400°C
B] 300°
C] 200°C
D] 100°C

126] What is the name of temperature measuring instrument?
A] Vapour pressure thermometer
B] Bimetalic thermometer

C] Radiation pyrometer

D] Thermoelectric pyrometer

127] Which instrument is used to measure temperatures of red hot metals up to 3000°C?

A] Radiation pyrometer

B] Thermoelectric pyrometer

C] Bimetal thermometer

D] Alcohol thermometer

128] Which type of heat transmission takes place through physical contact?

A] Conduction

B] Convection

C] Radiation

D] Reflection

129] Which kind of heat transmission takes places by up-ward flow?

A] Conduction

B] Convection

C] Radiation

D] Reflection

130] Which one is the radiation method of heat transmission?

A] An iron rod is heated with one of its end and heat transmitted to other end

B] Cold water goes to the bottom from top while on heating the water

C] On heating gases, heat transmitted to surroundings

D] The heat from sun travels through the space

131] What is called if the length of the solid expands when heated?

A] Linear expansion

B] Superficial expansion

C] Cubical expansion

D] Area expansion

132] What is the change in length per unit original length per degree rise in temperature is called?

A] Co-efficient of friction

B] Co-efficient of linear expansion

C] Co-efficient of superficial expansion

D] Co-efficient of cubical expansion

133] What is the unit of co-efficient of linear expansion?

A] Number /°C

B] Number /°C / meter length
C] Number /°C / mm length
D] Number /°C / cm length
134] What is term used for 2 x linear expansion?
A] Co-efficient of friction
B] Co-efficient of linear expansion
C] Co-efficient of superficial expansion
D] Co-efficient of cubical expansion
135] What is term called for 3 x linear expansion?
A] Co-efficient of friction
B] Co-efficient of linear expansion
C] Co-efficient of superficial expansion
D] Co-efficient of cubical expansion
136] What is the co-efficient of linear expansion of a rod if it is found to be 100 m long at 20°C and 100.14 m long at 100°C?
A] 1.75 x 10-4 / °C
B] 1.75 x 10-5 / °C
C] 1.75 x 10-6 / °C
D] 1.75 x 10-7 / °C
137] What is called for the amount of heat required to raise the temperature of unit mass of a substance through 1°C?
A] Sensible heat
B] Latent heat
C] Specific heat
D] Mixing of heat
138] How much quantity of heat is required? m = 120 litres t1 = 20°C t2 = 85°C S = 4.2 Q = ______ KJ
A] 32750 KJ
B] 32760 KJ
C] 32770 KJ
D] 32780 KJ
139] Calculate the amount of heat required to raise the temperature of 85.5 gm of sand from 20°C to 35°C specific heat of sand = 0.1.
A] 128.25 Joules
B] 125.28 Joules
C] 128.26 Joules
D] 126.28 Joules

140] What is the specific heat of the material if we require 510 calories to raise the temperature of 170 gm of material from 50°C to 80°C?

A] 0.1

B] 0.01

C] 1.1

D] 1.11

141] How much quantity of heat is required to raise the temperature of 300 grams of copper (sp.heat 0.092 cal/gram) from 25°C to 75°C in Kcal?

A] 138 Kcal

B] 1.38 Kcal

C] 207 Kcal

D] 2.07 Kcal

142] How much heat is absorbed by a copper ingot weighing 400 Kg is heated

from 40°C to 72°C for the purpose of forging? (sp.heat of copper is 0.09)

A] 1521 Kcal

B] 1251 Kcal

C] 1152 Kcal

D] 1215 Kcal

143] What is called for the materials that restricts heat flow by radiation, conduction and convection?

A] Conductors

B] Insulators

C] Ferrous

D] Non-ferrous

144] Which one is heat insulator?

A] Thermocole

B] Copper

C] Brass

D] Aluminium

145] Which one has the highest thermal conductivity?

B] Melting ice

C] Water

D] Steam

146] Which one of the following is not a property of heat insulating material?

A] Low conductivity

B] Resistance to fire
C] Less moisture absorption
D] Ductility
147] Which insulating material is most widely used in refrigerators?
A] Thermocole
B] Polyurethane
C] Glass wool
D] Cork sheet
148] Which one is a poor heat insulator?
A] Glass
B] Cork
C] Rubber
D] Saw dust
149] What is known for the temperature at which any solid melts into liquid?
A] Boiling point
B] Melting point
C] Latent heat of fusion
D] Latent heat of vaporisation
150] What is the melting point of aluminium?
A] 660°C
B] 680°C
C] 670°C
D] 620°C
151] What is the boiling point of aluminium?
A] 1897°C
B] 2519°C
C] 2469°C
D] 660°C
152] What is the boiling point of water?
A] 0°C
B] 32°C
C] 100°C
D] 212°C
153] What is the melting point of mercury?
A] -357°C
B] -209°C
C] -7.1°C

D] -38.72°C

154] What is the boiling point of mercury?

A] 357°C

B] 280°C

C] 759°C

D] 767°C

155] What is the ratio of force (or) thrust per unit area?

A] Work

B] Power

C] Pressure

D] Energy

156] What is the equivalent pascal value for 1 bar?

A] 105 pascal

B] 107 pascal

C] 103 pascal

D] 109 pascal

157] What is the SI unit of pressure?

A] Joule

B] Pascal

C] Bar

D] Newton

158] Which machine converts mechanical energy into electrical energy?

A] Battery

B] Generator

C] Heater

D] Iron box

159] Which is the unit of current?

A] Ampere

B] Volt

C] Ohm

D] Watt

160] Which is the unit of resistance?

A] Ampere

B] Volt

C] Ohm

D] Watt

161] What is the flow of electrons in any conductor?

A] Voltage
B] Current
C] Resistance
D] Power

162] Which property of a substance is opposing the flow of electric current?

A] Current
B] Voltage
C] Resistance
D] EMF

163] Which is very good conductor?

A] Copper
B] Cast iron
C] Wrought iron
D] Steel

164] Which is mineral insulator?

A] Glass
B] Quartz
C] Mica
D] Porcelain

165] What is the total resistance if three resistances of 3 ohms, 9 ohms and 5 ohms are connected in series?

A] 11 ohms
B] 7 ohm
C] 17 ohms
D] 1/17 ohms

168] Which is same in series connection of resistors in a circuit?

A] Current
B] Voltage
C] Resistance
D] Power

169] Which law states that at constant temperature the current passing through a closed circuit is directly proportional to the potential difference and inversely proportional to the resistance?

A] Ohm´s law
B] Lenz´s law
C] Newton´s law
D] Hooke´s law

170] What is the resistance? I = 11.5 Amps V = 380 Volts R = ________Ohms

A] 13 ohms

B] 23 ohms

C] 33 ohms

D] 43 ohms

171] What is the current? R = 50 Ohms 220 Volts I =________Amps

A] 4.1 Amps

B] 4.2 Amps

C] 4.3 Amps

D] 4.4 Amps

172] What is the voltage? R = 250 Ohms I = 0.44 Amps V = ______Volts

A] 100 Volts

B] 105 Volts

C] 108 Volts

D] 110 Volts

173] Which statement is correct according to ohm´s law?

A] I µ 1/V

B] I µ R

C] I µ V/R

D] I µ R/V

174] What is the filament resistance if a 6 volt bulb draws a current of 0.5 Amps?

A] 12 W

B] 10 W

C] 3 W

D] 1.2 W

175] How much watt second in 1 watt hour?

A] 1000 watt sec

B] 2000 watt sec

C] 3600 watt sec

D] 4000 watt sec

176] What is the power if an emf of one volt causes a current flow of 1ampere?

A] 1 watt

B] 1 kilowatt

C] 1 HP

D] 1 Kilowatt hour

178] How much power does it consumes if an electric heater draws a current of 10 amps at 200 volts?

A] 2000 watts

B] 2010 watts

C] 2020 watts

D] 2030 watts

179] What is the resistance of an electric iron if the rating of electric iron is 220 V and 500 watts?

A] 94.8 ohms

B] 95.8 ohms

C] 96.8 ohms

D] 97.8 ohms

180] What is the voltage of the immersion heater? P = 500 watts I = 2.27 Amps V = ______Volts

A] 200.3 volts

B] 210.3 volts

C] 220.3 volts

D] 230.3 volts

181] What is the unit of intensity of magnetic field?

A] wb/m

B] m/wb

C] Hertz

D] Coloumb

182] Which law states about electromagnetic induction?

A] Ohm´s law

B] Hooke´s law

C] Lenz´s law

D] Faraday´s law

183] What is the formual for induced emf?

A] B2L sinq volts

B] BL sinq volts

C] BLV sinq volts

D] B2V sinq volts

184] What does EMF stands for?

A] Electronic Magnetic Force

B] Electro Motive Force

C] Electro Magnetic Force

D] Electromated Force

185] Which is the example for statically induced emf?

A] Generator

B] Motor

C] Transformer

D] Refrigerator

186] Which is the example for dynamicallly induced Emf?

A] Motor

B] Generator

C] Car

D] Motor bike

187] Which is the unit electrical power?

A] Volts

B] Ohms

C] Watts

D] Ampere

188] What is the current Flow in the bulb? P = 550 watts R = 22 Ohms I = _______Amps

A] 2 Amps

B] 3 Amps

C] 4 Amps

D] 5 Amps

189] What is the power required? I = 0.455 Amps R = 484 Ohms P = ______Watts

A] 98.2 watts

B] 99.2 watts

C] 100.2 watts

D] 101.2 watts

190] What is the rated power if an adjustable resistor bears the following label 1.5 k ohms/ 0.08A?

A] 9.2 watts

B] 9.4 watts

C] 9.6 watts

D] 9.8 watts

191] How much voltage will be required to illuminate a 40 watts fluorescent lamp draws a current of 0.10 amperes?

A] 390 volts

B] 395 volts

C] 400 volts

D] 405 volts

192] How many hours will take for a 100 watts bulb to consume 1 kwh energy? W = 1 Kwh P = 100 Watts t = ______Hours

A] 10 hours

B] 12 hours

C] 18 hours

D] 24 hours

193] What is the area of a square whose side is 18 cm?

A] 26 cm2

B] 36 cm2

C] 72 cm2

D] 324 cm2

194] What is the diagonal of a square plate whose side is 28 cm? A] 39.29 cm | 39.29 cm

B] 39.39 cm

C] 39.49 cm

D] 39.59 cm

195] What is the side of a square whose area is 625 mm2?

A] 15 mm

B] 20 mm

C] 25 mm

D] 30 mm

196] What is the perimeter of a rectangle whose length and breadth are 20 cm and 18 cm?

A] 56 cm

B] 66 cm

C] 76 mm

D] 86 mm

197] What is the area of a rectangle, whose length and breadth are 10cm and 8cm respectively?

A] 75 cm2

B] 80 cm2

C] 85 cm2

D] 90 cm2

198] What is the area of a right angled triangle having a base 10 cm and height 5 cm?

A] 20 sq.cm

B] 25 sq.cm

C] 30 sq.cm

D] 35 sq.cm

199] What is the primeter of scalene. Triangle having sides of 40mm, 20mm and 28mm?

A] 68 mm

B] 78 mm

C] 88 mm

D] 98 mm

200] What is the area of an equilateral triangle of side 450 mm?

A] 856.82 cm2

B] 866.82 cm2

C] 876.82 cm2

D] 886.82 cm2

201] What is the area of a circle of diameter 50 cm?

A] 1932.5 cm2

B] 1942.5 cm2

C] 1952.5 cm2

D] 1962.5 cm2

202] What is the area of a (A) semicircle whose dia is 20 cm (d)?

A] 147.1 cm2

B] 157.1 cm2

C] 167.1 cm2

D] 177.1 cm2

203] What is the cross sectional area of a circular ring of D = 38 mm d = 32mm?

A] 320 mm2

B] 330 mm2

C] 340 mm2

D] 350 mm2

204] What is the area of a sector of a circle of radius 5 cm and its angle is 96°?

A] 20.39 cm2

B] 20.93 cm2

C] 20.89 cm2

D] 20.98 cm2

205] What is the formula for area and perimeter of a hexagon?

A] 3 x Ö3/4 a2 unit2 3a unit

B] 4 x Ö3/4 a2 unit2 4a unit

C] 5 x Ö3/4 a2 unit2 5a unit

D] 6 x Ö3/4 a2 unit2 6a unit

206] What is the area of an ellipse if the major and minor axes are 5 cm and 3 cm respectively?

A] 27 cm2

B] 37 cm2

C] 47 cm2

D] 57 cm2

207] Find the total surface area of cube whose side is 25 cm.

A] 3740 cm2

B] 3745 cm2

C] 3750 cm2

D] 3755 cm2

208] Find the total surface area of a cast iron bar whose length, width and height are 20m, 15m and 12m.

A] 1340 m2

B] 1440 m2

C] 1540 m2

D] 1640 m2

209] What is the formula for total surface area of a cylinder?

A] 2π r (h + r) unit2

B] π r (h + r) unit2

C] π rh unit2

D] 2π rh unit2

210] What is the volume of a rectangular tank of 30 m length, 20m width and 10m height?

A] 5900 m3

B] 6000 m3

C] 6100 m3

D] 6200 m3

211] What is volume of the cylinder whose radius is 7 cm and height 12 cm?

A] 1842 c.c

B] 1844 c.c

C] 1846 c.c

D] 1848 c.c

212] What is the volume of sphere of radius 7 cm?

A] 1436 cm3

B] 1463 cm3

C] 1346 cm3

D] 1636 cm3

213] What is the formula for finding volume of a hollow cylinder having outer radius ′R′ inner radius ′r′ and height ′h′?

A] π (R2 - r2) h unit3

B] π/3 (R2 - r2) h unit3

C] 2/3 π(R2 - r2) h unit3

D] 4/3 π (R2 - r2)h unit3

214] What is the capacity of a conical tank of radius 2 m and height 5m?

A] 11 m3 | 11 m3

B] 21 m3 | 21 m3

C] 31 m3 | 31 m3

D] 41 m3 | 41 m3

215] How many liters of water a cylindrical tank of radius 75 cm and height 100 cm can hold?

A] 1766.25 liters

B] 1767.25 liters

C] 1768.25 liters

D] 1769.25 liters

216] What is the total surface area of a cylinder having radius 2 metres and height 5 metres?

A] 86 sq.metre

B] 88 sq.metre

C] 90 sq.metre

D] 92 sq.metre

217] Find the curved surface area of a cylinder 10 cm dia and 20 cm height?

A] 620 cm2

B] 628 cm2

C] 630 cm2

D] 638 cm2

218] What is the name of the object?

A] Triangular prism

B] Frustum of a pyramid

C] Frustum of a cone

D] Hexagonal prism

219] What is the ratio between the distance moved by the effort to the distance moved by the load?

A] Mechanical advantage

B] Velocity ratio

C] Efficiency

D] Fulcrum

220] What is the mechanical advantage, if a load of 1000 kg is lifted by a simple machine and effort applied is 250 kg?

A] 6

B] 8

C] 3

D] 4

221] What is the velocity ratio of a wheel and axle if the radii of wheel and axle are 375 mm and 75 mm respectively?

A] 3

B] 4

C] 5

D] 6

222] What is the velocity ratio of a simple machine of a mass 120 kg is lifted to a height of 5 metres by a force of 60 kg moving 15 metre. Calculate velocity ratio?

A] 1

B] 2

C] 3

D] 4

223] What is the efficiency of a simple screw jack having velocity ratio is 314.2 and mechanical advantage is 220?

A] 0.6

B] 0.65

C] 0.7

D] 0.75

224] How much load is lifted if an effort of 25 kg is applied to a simple machine having velocity ratio of 4 and efficiency 75%?

A] 65 kg

B] 70 kg

C] 75 kg

D] 80 kg

225] What is the name of fixed or supporting point of a lever?

A] Mechanical advantage
B] Fulcrum
C] Effort
D] Load

226] What effort required to lift a load of 150 kg in a wheel and axle, if the velocity ratio is 2.5 and the efficiency of the machine is 75%?
A] 70 kg
B] 80 kg
C] 90 kg
D] 100 kg

227] What is the distance of the load from the fulcrum called?
A] Effort arm
B] Load arm
C] Power arm
D] Effort

228] Which is example for first order lever?
A] A wheel barrow
B] A pair of scissors
C] Fire tongs
D] Lime squeezer

229] Which is example for second order lever?
A] Common balance
B] A pair of scissors
C] Bottle opener
D] Human forearm

230] Which is example for third order lever?
A] Common balance
B] Forceps
C] A pair of scissors
D] Lime squeezer

231] Which type of levers is bell cranked lever?
A] Curved lever
B] 1st order lever
C] 2nd order lever
D] 3rd order lever

232] Which order lever is claw hammer?
A] 1st order lever
B] 2nd order lever

C] 3rd order lever
D] Curved lever
234] Which is equal to sinq?
A] Opposite Side/Hypotenuse
B] Hypotenuse/Opposite side
C] Adjacent Side/Hypotenuse
D] Hypotenuse/Adjacent side
235] What is equal to cosq?
A] Hypotenuse/Adjacent Side
B] Adjacent Side/Hypotenuse
C] Opposite side/Hypotenuse
D] Hypotenuse/Opposite Side
236] What is equal to tanq?
A] Opposite Side/Hypotenuse
B] Adjacent Side/Hypotenuse
C] Opposite Side/Adjacent Side
D] Adjacent side/Opposite side
238] What is the value of q if sinq = Ö3/2 ?
A] 30°
B] 45°
C] 60°
D] 90°
241] What is 1 + cot2q?
A] sec2q
B] cosec2q
C] cot2q
D] tan2q

242] What is the height of the wall where the ladder touches the wall if the ladder is 2.5 m long makes an angle of 60° with the ground?

A] 4.13 m
B] 4.23 m
C] 2.165 m
D] 4.43 m
243] What is the height of AC?
A] 1.732 m
B] 17.32 m
C] 173.2 m
D] 1732 m

244] What is the height of the building if a ladder at 45° touches the building placed 16 m from the base of the building?

A] 15 m

B] 16 m

C] 17 m

D] 18 m

245] What is the angle of elevation of the top of a light house of 15 m height seen at a point 15 m away from the base?

A] 30°

B] 45°

C] 60°

D] 90°

246] What is the angle of q?

A] 30°

B] 45°

C] 60°

D] 90°

247] What is the term for the object seen higher than eye level?

A] Angle of inclination

B] Angle of friction

C] Angle of elevation

D] Angle of depression

ANSWERS

1]C; 2]B; 3]B; 4]B; 5]C; 6]B; 7]A; 8]D; 9]B; 10]D; 11]B; 12]D; 13]B; 14]B; 15]B; 16]A; 17]A; 18]C; 19]B; 20]C; 21]A; 22]C; 23]D; 24]C; 25]A; 26]D; 27]B; 28]C; 29]C; 30]D; 31]B; 32]C; 33]A; 34]B; 35]D; 36]B; 37]B; 38]A; 39]C; 40]B; 41]C; 42]C; 43]C; 44]C; 45]B; 46]D; 47]A; 48]C; 49]A; 50]D; 51]C; 52]B; 53]D; 54]C; 55]A; 56]D; 57]C; 58]D; 59]D; 60]C; 61]A; 62]C; 63]C; 64]C; 65]B; 66]C; 67]B; 68]A; 69]A; 70]D; 71]D; 72]A; 73]D; 74]A; 75]D; 76]B; 77]C; 78]A; 79]A; 80]A; 81]B; 82]A; 83]D; 84]C; 85]D; 86]B; 87]B; 88]B; 89]D; 90]B; 91]B; 92]C; 93]B; 94]C; 95]B; 96]B; 97]A; 98]C; 99]A; 100]C; 101]C; 102]B; 103]C; 104]A; 105]A; 106]B; 107]B; 108]D; 109]B; 110]C; 111]D; 112]B; 113]B; 114]B; 115]A; 116]B; 117]D; 118]B; 119]A; 120]D; 121]D; 122]C; 123]A; 124]D; 125]B; 126]B; 127]A; 128]A; 129]B; 130]D; 131]A; 132]B; 133]A; 134]C; 135]D; 136]B; 137]C; 138]B; 139]A; 140]A; 141]B; 142]C; 143]B; 144]A; 145]A; 146]D; 147]B; 148]A; 149]B; 150]A; 151]B; 152]C; 153]D; 154]A; 155]C; 156]A; 157]B; 158]B; 159]A; 160]C; 161]B; 162]C; 163]A; 164]C; 165]C ; 166]B; 167]C;

168]A; 169]A; 170]C; 171]D; 172]D; 173]C; 174]A; 175]C; 176]A; 177]B; 178]A; 179]C ; 180]C; 181]A; 182]D; 183]C; 184]B; 185]C; 186]B; 187]C; 188]D; 189]C; 190]C; 191]C; 192]A; 193]D; 194]D; 195]C; 196]C; 197]B; 198]B; 199]C; 200]C; 201]D; 202]B; 203]B; 204]B; 205]D; 206]C; 207]C; 208]B; 209]A; 210]B; 211]C; 212]A; 213]A; 214]B; 215]A; 216]B; 217]B; 218]C; 219]B; 220]D; 221]C; 222]C; 223]C; 224]C; 225]B; 226]B; 227]B; 228]B; 229]C; 230]B; 231]A; 232]A; 233]D; 234]A; 235]B; 236]C; 237]D; 238]C; 239]C; 240]B; 241]B; 242]C; 243]C; 244]B; 245]B; 246]C; 247]C;

CHAPTER NINE

Friction MCQ

Scan for Theory Videos

1] Which is the law of friction?

A] Friction force is independent over the area and shape of contacting surfaces

B] Frictional force is inversely proportional to the normal reaction

C] Frictional force acts in the same direction of motion

D] Frictional force is not a dependent on nature of contacting surface

2] What is the direction of frictional force against a motional object?

A] Inclined to the object

B] Opposite to the object

C] Parallel to the object

D] Perpendicular to the object

3] Which force is directly proportional to the normal reaction between contacting surfaces?

A] Pulling force

B] Pushing force

C] Frictional force

D] Allied force

4] Which one of the following acts in between the wheels and roads, if vehicles are able to run on roads?

A] Friction

B] Corrosion

C] Erosion

D] Motion

5] Which is useful friction?

A] Rings in the cylinder

B] Crank shaft bearings

C] Wheel hub bearings

D] Brake shoe lining

6] Which is wasteful friction?

A] Rear axle gear

B] Tyres on the floor

C] Brake shoe lining

D] Clutch lining

7] Which is depends on the frictional force?

A] Type of metals

B] Contact surfaces

C] Quantity of the contacting metals

D] Quality of metals

8] How co-efficient of friction is expressed?

A] It is expressed as the ratio of force and area

B] It is the ratio between frictional force and normal reaction

C] It is the ratio between normal reaction and the mass of the object

D] It is expressed as the ratio of weight and normal reaction

10] Which symbol is used to denote co-efficient of friction?

A] α (Alpha)

B] μ (Meu)

C] β (Beta)

D] γ (Gamma)

11] What kind of friction is called if two objects are in contact at rest?

A] Sliding friction
B] Rolling friction
C] Static friction
D] Angular friction
12] Which is the correct statement?
A] Limiting friction is equal to sliding friction
B] Rolling friction is more than the sliding friction
C] Sliding friction is always less than limiting friction
D] Limiting friction is always less than sliding friction
15] What is the co-efficient of friction if the angle of friction isq?
A] Sin θ
B] Cos θ
C] Tan θ
D] Cot θ
17] What is the purpose of a lubricant?
A] To increase the pressure
B] To increase friction
C] To reduce friction
D] To reduce pressure
18] What type of lubricant is used in wick feed lubrication system
A] Lub-oil
B] Grease
C] Coolant
D] Cutting oil
19] Which lubrication system is provided with a ring oiler to splash lub-oil continuously around the parts?
A] Gravity feed system
B] Pressure feed system
C] Splash feed system
D] Force feed system
20] Which one is the three types of lubrication system in general use?
A] Force feed system, speed feed system, frictional feed system
B] Velocity feed system, Speed feed system, Frictional feed system
C] Gravity feed system, force feed system, splash feed system
D] Splash feed system, Frictional force system, Speed feed system
21] Which lubrication system employs oil holes in the machines?
A] Gravity feed system
B] Force feed system

C] Splash feed system

D] Velocity feed system

23] Which is used to reduce the friction in machine parts?

A] Kerosene

B] Petrol

C] Water

D] Lubricants

24] Which is the main purpose of using the lubricant oil in engine moving parts

A] To increase the efficiency

B] To reduce friction

C] To improve carrying capacity

D] To improve the durability

25] Which is the correct statement?

A] Lubricants acts to prevent corrosion

B] Lubricants acts as a seal

C] Lubricants acts as a fuel

D] Lubricants acts as a filter

26] What causes the efficiency of a machine by maintaining the lubrication?

A] Increases

B] Decreases

C] Remains same

D] Does not affected

29] Which way the coolant acts as a lubricant?

A] To carry away dust

B] To carry away the heat

C] To carry away moisture

D] To carry away dryness

30] What is the force required to move a body of mass 1000 kg if the co-efficient of friction is 0.4 (assume 1kg = 10 N)?

A] 4000 N

B] 400 N

C] 40 N

D] 4 N

31] What is the co-efficient of friction if a force of 30 N is required to move a body of mass 35 kg (Assume 1kg=10N)?

A] 8.57

B] 0.082

C] 0.0857

D] 0.0085

32] How much force is required to move an object weights 20 kg, if the value of m = 0.24?

A] 4.8 kg

B] 83.33 kg

C] 1.2 kg

D] 0.48 kg

33] What is weight of an object could be moved by a force of 30 kg if co-efficient of friction is 0.0125?

A] 80 kg

B] 2430 kg

C] 72000 kg

D] 2400 kg

34] What is the angle of inclination if a weight of 150 kg is in equilibrium and the value of m is 0.5773?

A] 30°

B] 45°

C] 60°

D] 90°

35] How much force is required to just slide a 20 kg object lying on a horizontal table if the m is 0.2? A] 2 kg

B] 3 kg

C] 4 kg

D] 5 kg

36] What is the force required to move a 20 kg object with a co-efficient of friction is 0.24?

A] 4.8 kg

B] 0.48 kg

C] 0.048 kg

D] 0.0048 kg

37] What is co-efficient of friction for pulling a load of 400 kg by a force of 40 kg?

A] 0.01

B] 0.2

C] 0.1

D] 0.02

38] How much will be the co-efficient of friction for moving a body of mass 80 kg by a force of 40 kg on a horizontal surface?

A] 0.05

B] 0.5

C] 0.65

D] 0.45

39] How much will be the weight of a body which will be moved by a horizontal force of 50 kg against a frictional resistance of 0.25?

A] 150 kg

B] 200 kg

C] 250 kg

D] 300 kg

40] What will be the approximate angle of inclination of an object if the co-efficient of friction m=0.84?

A] 60°

B] 45°

C] 40°

D] 30°

41] What is the work done to move a body of mass 60 kg to a distance of 5 meters, if the co-efficient if friction between body and the plane is 0.2?

A] 12 kg

B] 60 kg

C] 12 m-kg

D] 60 m-kg

42] How much will be the work done in moving a 10 kg object resing on a horizontal plane through a distance of 10 meter (assume m= 0.15)?

A] 1.5 m-kg

B] 15 m-kg

C] 0.15 m-kg

D] 150 m-kg

43] How much force is required to stop a vehicle of mass 1000 kg running on a road with coefficient of friction between the tyres and the road is 0.4?

A] 3000 kg

B] 450 kg

C] 350 kg

D] 400 kg

44] Which affects the centre of gravity of the object?

A] Weight
B] Mass
C] Density
D] Shape

45] What is the name of the point at which all the weight of the body concentrated?

A] Initial point
B] Centre of gravity
C] Centroid
D] Central point

46] Where the centre of gravity of a circle lies?

A] At its centre
B] Any where on its radius
C] Any where on its circumference
D] Any where on its diameter

47] What is the centre of gravity of a right circular cone from its base?

A] h/2
B] h/3
C] h/4
D] h/5

48] What is the centre of gravity of a rectangular body?

A] Longer side of rectangle
B] Shorter side of rectangle
C] At the point of intersection of its diagonals
D] At the corners

49] What is the centre of gravity of a solid hemisphere from its base?

A] 4r/5
B] 3r/8
C] 3r/4
D] r/2

50] What is the centre of gravity of a sphere?

A] At the centre
B] On the circumference
C] At the diameter
D] At the radius

51] Which state of equilibrium's example is A cone resting on its tip?

A] Stable
B] Neutral

C] Unstable

D] Horizontal

52] Which one of the following geometrical shape's centre of gravity lies from its base is 1/3 of its height?

A] Square

B] Rhombus

C] Triangle

D] Cone

53] Which state of equilibrium's example is, A cone resting on its base?

A] Un-stable

B] Neutral

C] Stable

D] Bothe A and B

CHAPTER TEN

Centre of gravity MCQ

Scan for Theory Videos

60] What is the centre of gravity of the cone base 10cm and height 50 cm?

A] 10.5 cm

B] 12.5 cm

C] 11.25 cm

D] 12.75 cm

61] What is the centre of gravity of a semi circle of diameter 12 cm?

A] 2.24 cm

B] 2.54 cm

C] 3.25 cm

D] 2.75 cm

62] Which formula is suitable for the area of a circle, whose diameter is (d)?

A] $\pi d^2 / 4$

B] πr

C] $2\pi r$

D] πd

63] What is the circumference of a semi circle?

A] $\pi r + 2r$

B] $\pi d / 4$

C] $2\pi r^2$

D] $\pi d^2 / 4$

64] What is the area of irregular shape by simpson's is rule?

A] $h/3\ [y_1 + y_7 + 4\ (y_2 + y_4 + y_6) + 2(y_3 + y_5]$

B] $h/2\ [y1 + y7]$

C] $h/3\ [y_2 + y_4 + y_6]$

D] $h/2\ [y_1 = y_7 + (y + y_5)]$

65] What is the name called biggest chord of the circle?

A] Arc

B] Diameter

C] Radius

D] Diagonal

66] What is the formula for circumference of a circle?

A] πr^2

B] $\pi d^2 / 4$

C] $2\pi r$

D] πr

67] What is the formula for area of the semi circle?

A] πr^2

B] $2\pi r$

C] πr

D] $\pi d^2 / 2$

CHAPTER ELEVEN

Area of cut out regular Surfaces and Irregular surfaces MCQ

Scan for Theory Videos

68] What is the formula for area of the circle?

A] $\pi d^2 / 2$

B] πr^2

C] $2\pi r$

D] $\pi d / 2$

74] What is the length of arc of a sector, whose perimeter is 64.8cm and radius is 12.4 cm?

A] 40 cm

B] 45 cm

C] 40.8 cm

D] 42 cm

75] What is the length of arc of the sector whose radius is 15 cm and the intended angle is 30°?

A] 7.85 cm

B] 7.25 cm

C] 6.75 cm

D] 6.85 cm

76] What is the area of the sector, if the diameter is 12 cm and the angle is 60°?

A] 18.0 cm^2

B] 17.75 cm^2

C] 19.00 cm^2

D] 18.84 cm^2

77] What is the formula for area of the segment of a circle?

A] Area of the sector - Area of the triangle

B] Area of the circle

C] Area of the sector

D] Area of the triangle - Area of the sector

78] What is the area of the circle, if the circumference of the circle is 44cm?

A] 128 cm^2

B] 130 cm^2

C] 154 cm^2

D] 129 cm^2

81] What is the radius of the circle if the angle of sector is 90° and the area of the circle is 196 cm2? A] 15.77 cm

B] 15 cm

C] 14.85 cm

D] 14.95 cm

82] What is the formula for perimeter of a sector?

A] 2l + r

B] l + 2r

C] πr^2

D] $2\pi r$

85] What is the area of the sector, whose diameter is 40 mm and angle is 120°?

A] 418.66 mm^2

B] 400.50 mm^2

C] 415.5 mm^2

D] 416.6 mm^2

86] What is the length of arc of a sector, whose radius is 15 cm and angle is 40°?

A] 9.75 cm

B] 9.8 cm

C] 10.60 cm

D] 10.4 cm

87] What is the length of arc of a sector whose radius is 3.6 cm and angle is 36°?

A] 2.10 cm

B] 2.26 cm

C] 22.6 cm

D] 21.0 cm

91] What is the area of the circle, whose diameter is 50 cm?

A] 1900 cm^2

B] 1950 cm^2

C] 1962.5 cm^2

D] 1960 cm^2

92] What is the name of the region of a circle between any two point on the circumference?

A] Arc

B] Segment

C] Sector

D] Chord

93] What is the radius of the circle, whose circumference is 440 cm?

A] 71.5 cm

B] 70 cm

C] 70.5 cm

D] 72.2 cm

94] What is the area of a circular surface if the radius is 14 cm?

A] 615.44 cm^2

B] 614.5 cm^2

C] 612.25 cm^2

D] 612.44 cm^2

95] What is the circumference of a circle whose diameter is 7 cm?

A] 22 cm

B] 44 cm

C] 25 cm

D] 21 cm

96] What is the radius of a circle whose diameter is 44 cm?

A] 44 cm

B] 22 cm

C] 23 cm

D] 20 cm

97] What is the diameter of the circle, if the area of the circle is 78.5cm^2?

A] 5 cm

B] 10 cm

C] 15 cm

D] 5.5 cm

98] What is the area of the circle if the radius is 10 cm?

A] 314 cm^2

B] 31.4 cm^2

C] 30.4 cm^2

D] 3.14 cm^2

99] What is the radius of the semicircle, if the circumference of the semicircle is 28.26 cm?

A] 5.49 cm

B] 6.49 cm

C] 8.5 cm

D] 8.75 cm

100] What is the diameter of the semicircle, if the circumference of the semicircle is 21.98 cm?

A] 8.55 cm

B] 8 cm

C] 7.55 cm

D] 7 cm

101] What is the area of the semicircle, if the diameter is 14 cm?

A] 70 cm^2

B] 76.93 cm^2

C] 75.06 cm^2

D] 86.93 cm^2

102] What is the diameter of the circle, if the area of the circle is 706.5cm^2?

A] 29 cm

B] 29.5 cm

C] 30 cm

D] 30.5 cm

103] What is the diameter of the circle, if the circumference is 31.4 cm?

A] 5 cm

B] 10 cm

C] 8 cm

D] 8.5 cm

CHAPTER TWELVE

Algebra MCQ

Scan for Theory Videos

112] What is the value of 14x+3y+25x+2y?

A] 17x + 27y

B] 16x + 28y

C] 39x + 5y

D] 44xy

113] What is the multiplication value of $5a^2b$ x $8a^5b^3$?

A] $40a^7b^4$

B] $40a^3b^2$

C] $40a^4b^7$

D] $40a^2b^3$

114] What is the simplified value of (3x + 15) / 5x + 25)

A] 5/3
B] 3/5
C] -5/3
D] -3/5
115] What is the value of x if 13+x =20?
A] 8
B] 7
C] 9
D] 13
116] What is the value of x, if x (120) = 960?
A] 6
B] 7
C] 8
D] 10
117] What is the formula for a^m x a^n?
A] a^{m+n}
B] a^{m-n}
C] a^{mn}
D] n.a^m
118] Which is the formula for a^m / a^n
A] a^{m+n}
B] a^{m-n}
C] $a^{m \times n}$
D] $(a^m)^n$
119] What is the value of any number raised to the power of 0?
A] 0
B] 1
C] -1
D] α
120] What is the value of 1 / a^m ?
A] a^m
B] a^{-m}
C] $\sqrt[m]{a}$
D] $\sqrt[a]{m}$
121] Which is equal to $(a^m)^n$?
A] a^{m-n}
B] a^{m+n}

C] $a^m/^n$

D] a^{mn}

122] What is the expanded form of $(a+b)^2$?

A] $a^2 + 2ab + b^2$

B] $a^2 - 2ab + b^2$

C] $a^2 + 2ab - b^2$

D] $-a^2 - 2ab + b^2$

123] What is the formula for $(a-b)^2$?

A] $a^2- 2ab + b^2$

B] $a^2 + 2ab + b^2$

C] $a^2 - 2ab - b^2$

D] $-a^2 - 2ab - b^2$

124] Which is equal to $(a+b)^2-(a-b)^2$?

A] 2ab

B] 3ab

C] 4ab

D] 5ab

125] What is the value of $a \times a^2 \times a^3 \times a^4$?

A] a^7

B] a^8

C] a^9

D] a^{10}

126] What is the value of $(a^5)^7$?

A] a^{35}

B] $a1^2$

C] a^21

D] a^{22}

127] What is the value of 625°?

A] 0

B] 1

C] 525

D] 25

128] What is the value of $1 / a^{-5}$?

A] a^5

B] $a^{-\ 5}$

C] 5a

D] -5a

129] What is the value of $5x^4 / 5x^3$?

A] $5x$
B] $5x^2$
C] x
D] $5x^{4/3}$
130] What is the subtracted value of $3x - 4x^2 + 2y^2$ from $4y^2 - 2x + 8x^2$?
A] $2y^2 - 5x + 12x^2$
B] $2y^2 + 5x - 12x^2$
C] $2y^2 - 5x - 12x^2$
D] $-2y^2 - 5x + 12x^2$
131] What is the value of adding (5x+2y), (4x - 7z) and (15z - 3y)?
A] 9x - y + 8z
B] x - 9y + 8z
C] x + 9y + 8z
D] 9x + y - 8z
132] What is the value of $12x^3y^2 / 4x^2y$?
A] 8xy
B] 16xy
C] 3xy
D] -3xy
133] What is the value of x, if 3 (2x - 4) = -4x + 28 ?
A] 4
B] 8
C] 6
D] 12
134] What is the value of x if (x + 2) / 2 = 19?
A] 38
B] 33
C] 35
D] 36
135] What is the value of x if 11x+4=37?
A] 2
B] 3
C] 4
D] 5
136] What is the value of $1/a^m$?
A] a^m
B] a-m
C] $\sqrt{a^m}$

D] a1

137] What is the value of am/n?

A] am-n

B] am+n

C] 1 / a^m

D] $\sqrt[n]{a^m}$

138] Which is the expansion of $a^3 + b^3$?

A] $(a-b)(a^2 + b^2 - ab)$

B] $(a+b)(a^2 + b^2 - ab)$

C] $a^3 + b^3 + 3ab(a+b)$

D] $a^3 - b^3 + 3ab(a-b)$

139] What is the expansion of $(a+b+c)^2$?

A] $a^2 + b^2 + c^2 + 2(ab + bc + ca)$

B] $a^2 + b^2 + c^2 - 2ab + 2bc + 2ca$

C] $a^2 + b^2 + c^2 + 2ab - 2bc + 2ca$

D] $a^2 - b^2 - c^2 + 2ab + 2bc + 2ca$

140] Which is expanded form of $a^3 - b^3$?

A] $(a+b)(a^2 - b^2 - ab)$

B] $(a-b)(a^2 + b^2 + ab)$

C] $(a-b)(a^2 - b^2 - ab)$

D] $(a-b)(a^2 - b^2 + ab)$

141] What is the value of $(6^3) / ((-3)^3)$?

A] 8

B] -8

C] 27

D] -27

142] What is the value of x^2-y^2 if $(x+y) = 9$, $(x - y) = 4$?

A] 13

B] 65

C] 36

D] 46

143] What is the value of 'X' if $x - y = 6$ and $x + y = 8$?

A] 5

B] 6

C] 7

D] 14

144] What is the value of a^2+b^2 if $a+b=9$ and $ab = 20$?

A] 121

B] -121
C] 41
D] -41
145] What is the value of ab if $(a+b)^2=36$ $(a-b)^2=24$?
A] 6
B] 4
C] 3
D] 2
146] What is the value of $x^3+3y^2x^2$ if x=3, y=2?
A] 135
B] 81
C] 54
D] 63
147] What are the three consecutive numbers if there sum is 42?
A] 11,12,13
B] 12,13,14
C] 13,14,15
D] 14,15,16

CHAPTER THIRTEEN

Basic Elasticity MCQ

Scan for Theory Videos

148] Which is elastic material?
A] Nylon
B] Polystyrenes
C] Celluloid
D] Polycarbonates
149] Which is thermo plastic material?
A] Butyl rubber
B] Nylon
C] Neoprene
D] Vinyl polymers

150] What is the maximum percentage of stretch of its original length is allowable for elastic materials?

A] 100%

B] 200%

C] 300%

D] 400%

151] What is the ratio between the change in dimension to its original dimension of the substance? A] Stress

B] Strain

C] Poisson's ratio

D] Factor of safety

152] What is the unit of strain?

A] Kg/cm^2

B] $Newton/metre^2$

C] Metre

D] No unit

153] What is the ratio of change in length to original length?

A] Linear strain

B] Lateral strain

C] Volumetric strain

D] Poisson's ratio

154] What is the ratio between lateral strain and longitudinal strain?

A] Hooks law

B] Young's modulus

C] Bulk modulus

D] Poisson's ratio

155] Which symbol is used to express change in length?

A] L

B] ?l

C] I

D] e

156] Which one is the ratio of stress?

A] Load and area

B] Load and direction

C] Load and diameter

D] Load and time

157] Which force acts on rivets?

A] Tensile force

B] Compressive force

C] Shear force

D] Bending force

159] What is the formula for bulk modulus?

A] Tensile stress/Tensile strain

B] Compressive stress/Compressive strain

C] Volumetric stress/Volumetric strain

D] Shear stress/Shear strain

160] Which law states that within elastic limit stress is directly proportional to strain?

A] Newtons law

B] Hooks law

C] Joules law

D] Charles law

162] What is the term used for maximum stress attained by a material before rupture?

A] Tensile stress

B] Compressive stress

C] Working stress

D] Ultimate stress

163] What is the ratio between ultimate stress to working stress?

A] Bulk modulus

B] Young's modulus

C] Factor of safety

D] Modulus of rigidity

164] What is the ratio of ultimate load to area of original cross section?

A] Factor of safety

B] Yield point

C] Ultimate stress

D] Youngs modulus

166] What is the ratio of shear stress to shear strain?

A] Modulus of elasticity

B] Modulus of rigidity

C] Bulk modulus

D] Yield point

167] What is the ratio between stress and strain?

A] Yield point

B] Factor of safety

C] Youngs Modulus

D] Poisson's ratio

168] Which force acts on crank shaft?

A] Shear stress

B] Torsional stress

C] Tensile stress

D] Compressive stress

169] Which is thermosetting plastic?

A] Vinyl polymers

B] Polystyrenes

C] Celluloid

D] Melamine resins

170] What force will be required to punch a hole of 10 mm dia in a 1 mm thick plate, if the allowable shear stress is $50N/mm^2$? ($\pi = 22/7$)

A] 1757 N

B] 1575 N

C] 1571.4 N

D] 1577 N

171] What is the tensile stress if a square rod of 10 mm side is tested for a tensile load of 1000 kg?

A] 1 kg/mm^2

B] 10 kg /mm^2

C] 100 kg/mm^2

D] 1000 kg/mm^2

172] What is the tensile strain if a force of 3.2 KN is applied to a bar of original length 2800 mm extends the bar by 0.5 mm?

A] 0.0001786

B] 0.0001687

C] 0.0001867

D] 0.0001968

173] How much strain is developed in an iron rod of 1 metre length gets elongated by 1 cm, if a force of 100 kg is applied at one end?

A] 0.1

B] 0.01

C] 0.001

D] 0.0001

174] What is the youngs modulus if a wire of 2m long, 0.8 mm2 in cross section increases its length by 1.6 mm on suspension of 8 kg weight from it?

A] 1.25 kg/mm^2
B] 12.5 kg/mm^2
C] 125 kg/mm^2
D] 12500 kg/mm^2

175] What is the safe stress if the ultimate stress of a material is 35 kg/mm^2 and factor of safety is 5?

A] 0.143
B] 0.7
C] 1.43
D] 7

CHAPTER FOURTEEN

Heat Treatment MCQ

Scan for Theory Videos

177] What are the various types of heat treatment processes?

A] Annealing, Normalising, Hardening and Tempering

B] Normalising, Heating, Cooling and Painting

C] Hardening, Soaking, Painting and Packing

D] Tempering, Cooling, Packing and Solling

178] What is the process of heat treatment?

A] The process of heating and cooling to change the structure and properties

B] The process of heating to change the dimensions

C] The process of cooling to measure the dimensions

D] The process of heating and bending as per our requirement

179] What are the various stages of heat treatment?

A] Heating, Cooling and Quenching

B] Quenching, Cooling and Heating

C] Heating, Soaking and Quenching

D] Soaking, Quenching and Cooling

180] What is the name of the structure formed, if a steel is heated for about 723°C?

A] Cementide

B] Austenite

C] Martensite

D] Ferrite

181] Which heat treatment process is done to refine the grain structure of the steel?

A] Annealing

B] Normalising

C] Hardening

D] Tempering

182] What is the name of heat treatment process done to relieve strain and stress?

A] Normalising

B] Annealing

C] Hardening

D] Tempering

183] Which process produce equilibrium conditions?

A] Annealing and Hardening

B] Normalising and Tempering

C] Annealing and Normalising

D] Normalising and Tempering

184] Which process steel is heated in a carbonaceous atmosphere for the penetration of carbon?

A] Case hardening

B] Nitriding

C] Carburising

D] Induction hardening

185] Which is the suitable nitriding process for all alloyed and unalloyed steels?

A] Silver nitriding

B] Nitriding in salt-bath

C] Nitriding in Quenching tank

D] Gas nitriding

186] What is the name of the heat treatment process, where the metal is heated and quenched in water or oil?

A] Hardening

B] Normalising and Tempering

C] Annealing

D] Tempering

187] Which is a kind of surface hardening process?

A] Cementide

B] Ferrite

C] Nitriding

D] Tempering

188] How much time is allowed normally in soaking zone for a 10mm thick metal piece while hardening?

A] 5 minutes

B] 10 minutes

C] 15 minutes

D] 20 minutes

189] What is colour of a metal piece when heated to 250°C while doing the tempering process?

A] Blue

B] Brown

C] Purple

D] Pale

190] What is the purpose of tempering a steel?

A] To reduce the brittleness

B] To remove the ductility

C] To increase the hardness

D] To increase the brittleness

CHAPTER FIFTEEN

Profit and Loss MCQ

Scan for Theory Videos

191] What is discount?
A] Selling price is less than Cost price
B] Selling price is greater than Cost price
C] The reduction given to the selling price of a product
D] Selling price + discount
192] What is a profit?
A] Selling price - Cost price
B] Cost price - Selling price
C] Selling price + Cost price
D] Cost price + Selling price
193] What is the term, if an article is purchased?

A] Selling price

B] Cost price

C] Margin price

D] Discount price

194] What is the expanded form of S.P?

A] Selected Price

B] Special Price

C] Selling Price

D] Super Price

195] Which is the short form of profit and loss statement?

A] P & L

B] PR & LS

C] PRO & LOS

D] L & P

196] What is denoted as 'I'?

A] Principal

B] Interest

C] Rate

D] Year

197] How the 'Principal' is denoted in simple interest calculation?

A] 'P'

B] 'I'

C] 'R'

D] 'n'

200] How the years is denoted in simple interest calculations?

A] P

B] I

C] n

D] r

201] How the profit / gain is expressed?

A] ?

B] $

C] %

D] *

206] What is the profit amount, if the i - phone cost price is Rs.50000/- and selling price is Rs.70000/-?

A] Rs. 2000/-

B] Rs. 10000/-

C] Rs. 20000/-

D] Rs. 50000/-

207] What is the selling price, if the profit is 5% for a computer table bought at Rs.1150/- with Rs.50/- as a transport charge?

A] 1160

B] 1620

C] 1060

D] 1260

208] What is the cost price if the product is sold at ? 572 with a profit of ? 72?

A] ? 500

B] ? 1000

C] ? 644

D] ? 472

209] What is the profit % if the cost price of 16 bolts is equal to the selling price of 12 bolts?

A] 13.33

B] 23.33

C] 33.33

D] 43.33

210] What is the selling price if the cost price is Rs.7282/- with a profit of Rs.208?

A] Rs.7074

B] Rs.7698

C] Rs.7290

D] Rs.7490

211] What is the interest earned, if the principal is Rs.12000/- becomes to an amount of Rs.15600/-? A] Rs.2600

B] Rs.3600

C] Rs.4600

D] Rs.5600

212] What is the principal amount deposited, if the maturity proceeds to an amount of Rs.25000/- and interest earned Rs.6000/-?

A] Rs.31000/-

B] Rs.19000/-

C] Rs.20000/-

D] Rs.25000/-

213] What is the interest earned, if the principal is for Rs.12500/- maturity becomes to a amount of Rs.17500/-?

A] Rs.30000

B] Rs.25000

C] Rs.5000

D] Rs.5500

214] What is the matured amount for the deposit of Rs.5000/- and the simple interest earned for Rs.500/-?

A] Rs.4500

B] Rs.5500

C] Rs.6000

D] Rs.6500

215] What is the simple interest for the principal amount of Rs.100000 at 10% per annum for 1 year period?

A] Rs.1000/-

B] Rs.5000/-

C] Rs.50000/-

D] Rs.10000/-

216] What is the compounded annual interest, for a loan amount of Rs.80000/- at 10% per annum for a period of 2 years?

A] Rs.16800/-

B] Rs.92400/-

C] Rs.96800/-

D] Rs.94800/-

217] What is the compounded amount, if the principal of Rs.30000/- and interest earned at 7% per annum is Rs.4347?

A] Rs.30347/-

B] Rs.32347/-

C] Rs.33347/-

D] Rs.34347/-

218] What is the difference between the simple and the compound interest amount at 5% per annum for 2 years on a principal of Rs.20000/-?

A] Rs.5

B] Rs.25

C] Rs.50

D] Rs.55

219] What is the maturity amount if Rs.20000 is deposited at 5% compound interest per annum for 2 years?

A] Rs.22000
B] Rs.22050
C] Rs.22500
D] Rs.25000

220] What is the compound interest on a principal of Rs.25000/- after 3 years at the rate of 12% per annum?
A] Rs. 9000
B] Rs.9720
C] Rs.10123.20
D] Rs.10483.20

221] What is the other term used for reference table?
A] Dictionary
B] Biography
C] Bibliography
D] Information Table

222] Which hand book referred by machine engineer?
A] Parry's cheorikal
B] CRC
C] Mark standard
D] Oxford Dictionary

223] What is a hand book?
A] Model book of various works
B] Type of reference work or other collection of instruction
C] Design book of latest works
D] Dictionary of materials

224] Which standard schedule of rates to be considered for estimation?
A] Standard schedule of rates of the last year
B] Standard schedule of rates of the average of the last 10 years
C] Standard schedule of rates of the average of last 5 years
D] Standard schedule of rates of the current year

225] What is an over estimate?
A] When an estimate is exceeded to actual estimate
B] When an estimate is fell short of the actual estimate
C] When an estimate perfectly matches the actual estimate
D] No work started as per estimate

226] What is a under estimate?
A] No work started as per estimate
B] An estimate perfectly matches with actual

C] An estimate is fell short of the actual estimate

D] An estimate is exceeded the actual estimate

227] What is the term used for the method of calculating various quantities and expenditure on a particular job or process?

A] Estimation

B] Drawing

C] Specification

D] Plan

228] What is the main factor to be considered while preparing a detailed estimate?

A] Shape of material

B] Brand of the materials

C] Quantity, availability and transportation of materials

D] Location of material

229] Which authority publishes schedule of rates?

A] Individual

B] Corporate

C] Partnership firm

D] Government department

230] What is the name of a booklet, the rates of various terms are indicated?

A] Price bank

B] Price bunch

C] Price tag

D] Price catalogue

231] What is the term, for the details of materials, brand name, grade of quality, rating of current and voltage etc.?

A] Drawing

B] Specification of materials

C] Raw materials

D] Price catalogue

232] What is the use of engineering drawing?

A] For estimation of material and execution of work

B] For colourful appearance

C] For reducing the cost

D] For increasing the cost

233] What is the other term of pocket reference in engineering works?

A] Hand tool

B] Hand book
C] Good book
D] New book
234] Which one is related to estimation of work?
A] Bill of material
B] Packing
C] Information table
D] Hand book
235] What is a total cost?
A] Raw material cost only
B] Machining cost only
C] Raw materials cost and machining cost
D] Advertisement cost only
236] Who prepares the cost of estimation?
A] Operator
B] Quality Inspector
C] Estimator
D] Draughts man
237] Which one is included in machining estimation sheet?
A] Transport cost
B] Advertisement cost
C] Raw material cost
D] Tax
238] What is the minimum permissible size of aluminium wire used in estimation?
A] 1.5 sq.mm
B] 2.5 sq.mm
C] 5 sq.mm
D] 3.5 sq.mm
239] What is the minimum permissible area of conductor (U/G cable) for three and half cores cable? A] 25 sq.mm
B] 50 sq.mm
C] 5 sq.mm
D] 100 sq.mm
240] Which one is the most reliable estimate?
A] Preliminary estimate
B] Plinth area estimate
C] Cube rate estimate

D] Detailed estimate

241] Which IE rules are to be verified on completion of wiring on any new installation?

A] IE Rules, 1956

B] IE Rules, 1960

C] IE Rules, 1961

D] IE Rules, 1967

242] What describes the detailed specification for the item of work?

A] Quality, Quantity, Workmanship, Method of execution

B] Colour

C] Tax, Transport, Overhead expenses

D] Maintenance, Stock, Cost

243] Which of the impurity in cast iron makes it hard and brittle?

A] Silicon

B] Sulphur

C] Manganese

D] Phosphorus

244] What cables are used for 132KV lines?

A] High tension

B] Super tension

C] Extra high tension

D] Extra super voltage

245] Which specification is other than general specification?

A] Brief specification

B] Bulk specification

C] Detailed specification

D] Main specification

246] What percentage of water absorbed by a good building stone?

A] Less than 10%

B] Less than 20%

C] Less than 8%

D] Less than 5%

247] What is the relative permittivity of rubber?

A] Between 2 and 3

B] Between 5 and 6

C] Between 8 and 10

D] Between 12 and 14

248] What is the weight of the iron ball has volume of 250 cc and density 7.5 gm/cc?

A] 1750 gram

B] 1875 gram

C] 1975 gram

D] 1785 gram

249] What is the weight of a rectangular block of a cost iron of 250cm X 20cm X 8cm (density of cast iron is 7.8 gm/cm^3)?

A] 312 kg

B] 372 kg

C] 410 kg

D] 525 kg

250] What is the total estimation cost for making the component of 8 drilled hole dia 10 mm and 4 Numbers of M6 taps in the plate, if Rs.8/- per drilled holes and Rs.12 per drill and tap?

A] Rs.102

B] Rs.100

C] Rs.112

D] Rs.110

251] What is the estimation of milling cost of a rectangular block size 100 X 80 X60 mm, if cost of the milling is Rs.2/sq.cm?

A] Rs.652/-

B] Rs.752/-

C] Rs.572/-

D] Rs.960/-

252] What is the total wattage in a room if 2 tube lights of 50W rating, 2 fans of 80W rating, 2 numbers of light points of 60W rating, one fan point of 60W rating and one 3 pin socket of 100W rating?

A] 340 W

B] 440 W

C] 540 W

D] 640 W

253] What is the total labour charges for a particular wiring work completed in 2 days by one electrician and one helper.(Electrician @ ?800/ day and helper @ ? 400/day)

A] Rs. 2000

B] Rs. 2400

C] Rs. 3000

D] Rs. 1400

254] What is the total cost of painting of a class room including ceiling, if the size of length is 6m, breadth is 5m and height is 4m. (Painting + labour cost Rs.150/- per sq.m)

A] Rs.15000/-

B] Rs.16700/-

C] Rs.17700/-

D] Rs.18700/-

255] What is the total cost to assemble 10 personal computer systems, spares cost as given for one system] 1 TB hard disc Rs.4500/-, Intel i3 mother board Rs.7000/-, SMPS Rs.2500/-, monitor Rs.6000/-, keyboard Rs.1000/-, other material cost (Switches, USB, Cables etc.,) Rs.6500/-?

A] Rs.275000/-

B] Rs.250000/-

C] Rs.225000/-

D] Rs.265000/-

256] What is the total construction cost of a house construction area of 3000 sq.ft. (cost of construction Rs.2000/- per sq.ft including material and labour)?

A] Rs.30,000,000

B] Rs.60,00,000

C] Rs.6,00,000

D] Rs.6,000,000

257] What is the total cost of Air-conditioners installed in a college, 40 class room-each 1 Air-conditioner, Computer lab 5 Air- conditioners and conference hall 5 Air-conditioners (Cost of one air conditioner Rs.30000/- including installation)?

A] Rs.10 lakhs

B] Rs. 20 lakhs

C] Rs. 12 lakhs

D] Rs. 15 lakhs

ANSWERS

1]A; 2]B; 3]C; 4]A; 5]D; 6]A; 7]B; 8]B; 9]D; 10]B; 11]C; 12]C; 13]B; 14]B; 15]C; 16]D; 17]C; 18]A; 19]C; 20]C; 21]A; 22]B; 23]D; 24]B; 25]A; 26]A; 27]C; 28]C; 29]B; 30]A; 31]C; 32]A; 33]D; 34]A; 35]C; 36]A; 37]C; 38]B; 39]B; 40]C; 41]D; 42]B; 43]D; 44]B; 45]B; 46]A; 47]C; 48]C; 49]B; 50]A; 51]C; 52]C; 53]C; 54]A; 55]C; 56]B; 57]A; 58]B; 59]C; 60]B; 61]B; 62]A; 63]A; 64]A; 65]B; 66]C; 67]D; 68]B; 69]C; 70]A; 71]B; 72]D; 73]C;

74]A; 75]A; 76]D; 77]A; 78]C; 79]D; 80]C; 81]A; 82]B; 83]D; 84]B; 85]A; 86]D; 87]B; 88]D; 89]A; 90]B; 91]C; 92]B; 93]B; 94]A; 95]A; 96]B; 97]B; 98]A; 99]A; 100]C; 101]B; 102]C; 103]B; 104]B; 105]B; 106]C; 107]A; 108]B; 109]C; 110]D; 111]D; 112]C; 113]A; 114]B; 115]B; 116]C; 117]A; 118]B; 119]B; 120]B; 121]D; 122]A; 123]A; 124]C; 125]D; 126]A; 127]B; 128]A; 129]C; 130]A; 131]A; 132]C; 133]A; 134]D; 135]B; 136]B; 137]D; 138]B; 139]A; 140]B; 141]B; 142]C; 143]C; 144]C; 145]C; 146]A; 147]C; 148]A; 149]D; 150]C; 151]B; 152]D; 153]A; 154]D; 155]B; 156]A; 157]C; 158]C; 159]C; 160]B; 161]A; 162]D; 163]C; 164]C; 165]A; 166]B; 167]C; 168]B; 169]D; 170]C; 171]B; 172]A; 173]B; 174]D; 175]D; 176]B; 177]A; 178]A; 179]C; 180]B; 181]B; 182]B; 183]C; 184]C; 185]B; 186]A; 187]C; 188]A; 189]B; 190]A; 191]C; 192]A; 193]B; 194]C; 195]A; 196]B; 197]A; 198]A; 199]C; 200]C; 201]C; 202]A; 203]B; 204]D; 205]D; 206]C; 207]D; 208]A; 209]C; 210]D; 211]B; 212]B; 213]C; 214]B; 215]D; 216]A; 217]D; 218]C; 219]B; 220]C; 221]D; 222]C; 223]B; 224]D; 225]A; 226]C; 227]A; 228]C; 229]D; 230]D; 231]B; 232]A; 233]B; 234]A; 235]C; 236]C; 237]C; 238]A; 239]B; 240]D; 241]A; 242]A; 243]B; 244]D; 245]C; 246]D; 247]A; 248]B; 249]A; 250]C; 251]B; 252]C; 253]B; 254]C; 255]A; 256]B; 257]D; 258]D; 259]B;

www.ingramcontent.com/pod-product-compliance
Ingram Content Group UK Ltd.
Pitfield, Milton Keynes, MK11 3LW, UK
UKHW021911190726
13853UKWH00002B/618

9 798887 497945